799.2

ROUGH SHOOTING IN IRELAND

To Margaret and Susan

ROUGH SHOOTING IN IRELAND

Douglas Butler

MERLIN UNWIN BOOKS

First published in the UK by Merlin Unwin Books, 2006

Published by:
Merlin Unwin Books
Palmers House
7 Corve Street
Ludlow
Shropshire SY8 1DB
U.K.

www.merlinunwin.co.uk

Designed and set in Sabon by Merlin Unwin Books
Printed by Compass Press

ISBN 1 873674 89 9
ISBN 978 1 873674 89 5

CONTENTS

ACKNOWLEDGEMENTS

A lot of people have helped me with the preparation of this book. I am indebted to Imelda Grauer, Seamus Butler and Rupert Butler for supplying the many photographs. My thanks too, to all the sportsmen who make an appearance on these pages. Philip Walsh, John Condon, Anthony O'Halloran and Paul Butler deserve special mention. They went uncomplainingly about their shooting whilst being pursued relentlessly by at least one photographer.

Michael Gately and Father Matt Glynn showed me many kindnesses and allowed Imelda to take photographs on their shoots in the North Slob in County Wexford. To both my grateful thanks.

Thanks also to Merlin Unwin and Karen McCall for guiding me through the mysteries of the publishing world. They have been very helpful and supportive.

REFERENCES

Butler, D. and Whelan, J., *The release and survival of the Red-legged Partridge (Alectoris Rufa) in Ireland*, 1987, Journal XII World Pheasant Association, 1986-1987

Butler, D., *The incidence of lead shot ingestion by wildfowl in Ireland*, 1990, Irish Naturalists Journal Vol. 23, No. 8, 309-313

Cummins, J., *Woodcock research in Ireland*, 1974, Unpublished report

Fitter, R.S.R., *The ark in our midst*, 1959, Collins, London

Lever, C., *The naturalised animals of the British Isles*, 1977, Hutchinson, London

A report on the status of game shooting and related matters, 1993, National Association of Regional Game Councils

Robertson, P.A., *The release and survival of hand reared pheasants on an unkeepered estate in Ireland*, 1986, The Game Conservancy Annual Review

Introduction

This is not a book about the rights and wrongs of history. Nor is it intended to be any form of social commentary. However, to understand the shooting scene in Ireland in the 21st century, it is necessary to probe a little into both the recent and not-so-recent past.

Ireland, with its heather-covered uplands, slow-flowing rivers with broad flood plains and forests, once of oak but now predominantly the abominable Sitka, possesses habitats for game which have all but disappeared over large tracts of Western Europe. Add the benefits that accrue from the proximity of the Atlantic and you have a country well-suited to the wintering requirements of both migratory and native birds.

When, centuries ago, the land of Ireland was divided amongst the officer-classes of a conquering alien power, the demands of the hunting field were not neglected. As well as embracing a more-than-adequate acreage of prime agricultural land, each estate was so ordered that, where possible, there was a river well-stocked with trout and salmon and, equally important, a large tract of scrub, forest and mountain. In those remote hunting paradises a considerable number of hunting lodges or their decaying remains are still to be seen. Out on the mountains the crumbling remnants of grouse butts bear eloquent testimony to what once was.

For those landlords of old the abundance of game of all species must have been a joy to behold. For, remember, they and they alone, were

Greenland white-fronts over the North Slob in County Wexford. Nearly half of the world's population winters here.

1

privileged to experience the passion of the chase. So plentiful was game that a flourishing export trade existed and lasted into the early years of the 20th century.

But all things change. Well before the 19th century had run its course the era of the great estates was coming to an end. No people remain a subject people forever and the people of Ireland finally laid claim for the return of that which was rightfully theirs. Starting in the 1880s a long series of Land Acts gradually returned ownership of the land of Ireland to the people of Ireland. Tenant farmers, after generations, were to become owner-occupiers.

Political change rarely, if ever, follows a smooth and peaceful pathway. Those years of change were, inevitably, turbulent ones as the new order replaced the old. Game, which had been held in high esteem by the landlord classes, and which had been carefully tended by small armies of gamekeepers, held little interest for most of their successors. The Land Acts redistributed several hundred thousand holdings, many no more than a few acres in extent, and the new owners had rather more important things on their minds than the needs of grouse and pheasant. Being an owner rather than a tenant made precious little difference when it came to the reality of tearing a living from an often unwilling soil.

As to the fate of the sporting rights associated with the old estates, there was little uniformity of treatment from Land Act to Land Act. In some cases the landlord, now bereft of his estate, managed to retain his sporting rights. In other cases they were passed to an agent living outside the country. Some of the Land Acts transferred the sporting rights to the new owner; others simply made no mention of them. In some of the later Acts the fledgling Irish State retained the sporting rights.

To the present day there are parts of Ireland in which, if the truth be known, no one knows who owns the sporting rights. A case in which I was personally involved will give an indication of both the complexity and hopelessness of the situation.

We were trying to establish the ownership of a certain mountain in order to establish a grouse restoration project. After an avalanche of legal correspondence we discovered that a certain descendant of a certain landlord had been given the rights in the 1930s for 'three generations'. This gentleman could not be traced. It was as if he had been removed from the face of the earth by aliens. To compound our difficulty we could not find a legal eagle prepared to tell us what a 'generation' precisely meant in law.

In the absence of evidence to the contrary it is tacitly assumed that the farmer in residence owns the rights whether or not they are actually written into his title deeds. Indeed, it would be an extremely foolish son of the gun who presumed to tell a landowner that he did not own the sporting rights of his lands and that, in consequence, the said son of the gun intended to shoot away. Such is not the stuff of political correctness in rural Ireland.

PARTRIDGE AND GROUSE POPULATIONS IN IRELAND

As the years of the 20th century rolled by, game bird populations came under ever-increasing levels of threat. Two species, the grey partridge and the red grouse, were already in trouble. As far back as the 1880s, despite the best ministering of the gamekeeping profession, a decline in partridge numbers had become apparent. The reasons for this are unclear. It was hardly a matter of habitat loss as farm structure and farming practices had remained largely unchanged. It is my personal belief that a small yet subtle change in climate played a significant role. Cool, damp conditions and an accompanying lack of essential insects may well have resulted in high levels of chick mortality.

Whilst Irish red grouse populations rarely equalled those of northern England and eastern Scotland, very substantial bags were recorded when breech loading shotguns appeared in the 19th century. Then, as with partridge, the last of the landlords realised that grouse numbers were also on the decline.

For both species the same remedy was applied: importation. In the case of the grey partridge the focus was turned on Hungary, a country renowned for its teeming partridge population where, in those far off years, the annual bag was being counted in millions. So widespread were these introductions in the latter years of the 19th century that the bird became commonly known as the Hungarian partridge.

Initially these efforts appear to have reversed the decline but it was not

to last. By the 1930s the Irish grey partridge was once more in trouble.

The importation of red grouse as a means of remedying decline probably never reached the levels recorded for the grey partridge. Nevertheless birds were released in many counties. These included Galway and Mayo. Best documented are the releases of grouse on the Wicklow hills in the early years of the 20th century. For a number of years birds were caught up in Yorkshire and Perthshire and brought to Wicklow, a county with probably the best heather in Ireland. The resulting story was similar to that of the partridge. These introductions initially had a beneficial effect and this was reflected in the size of the annual bag. But then it was the all-too-familiar story.

Once more the grouse was in decline.

Another almost immediate consequence of the break up of the great estates was a rapid decline in the number of gamekeepers. By the 1920s, with a few honourable exceptions, the profession had ceased to exist in Ireland. The resulting chain reaction was quite predictable. Predator numbers exploded, release programmes became the exception rather than the rule and work on habitat maintenance ground to a halt. Inevitably game stocks suffered.

The 1940s and 1950s saw little improvement. The grouse in particular was to suffer further declines in the face of human activity. The young republic needed timber and sources of rural employment. In consequence an ambitious programme of afforestation was set in progress. Unfortunately very many of these new plantations were sited on the lower flanks of mountains, roughly up to one thousand feet, areas that traditionally produced the most nutritious heather.

So was lost much prime grouse habitat. To make matters worse, no thought was given to leaving some of the lower ground unplanted so that grouse would have some refuge when the ferocity of winter laid waste the higher ground.

A new flight pond just dug out at the top of our bog. It is now well colonised with vegetation and this year it attracted wigeon, as well as mallard and teal.

RIGHT
An adult cock pheasant is released in early spring.

Whilst the coming of the forestry took its toll on the mountain grouse this was nothing compared to the fate that awaited the populations of the lowland heather bogs. Ever-increasing levels of turf extraction, cutting down to the very bedrock, devastated the heather and sent the lowland grouse hurtling to sure and certain extinction.

But if it was all bad news for resident game birds, the same could not be said for the woodcock and the snipe, the wigeon and the teal. I have referred to the benign influence of the Atlantic. From the frozen wastes of northern Canada and Greenland, from Iceland, Scandinavia, the Baltic States and further east, a trickle of migrants in late summer becomes a torrent as the weeks of autumn pass. All have a single purpose, to take full advantage of the natural bounty provided by the waters and moist soils of Ireland.

The 1940s and 1950s were not, in economic terms, a happy period in Irish history. The reality of emigration cast its long shadow over every village and townland. Not surprisingly, therefore, the number of people who had the time and the wherewithal to shoot was not large. This being said there was still a sufficiency of game to meet the needs of local sportsmen. Expectations were not high and most were well satisfied with a brace of cock pheasants or a few woodcock in the bag. Then, as the 1950s gave way to the 1960s interest, in the sport began to expand. In a number of counties enlightened individuals began to realise that drastic action was required if the sport were to flourish. Order and discipline had to become the order of the day. And so the gun club movement was born.

An Irish gun club is something unique. Essentially, with the permission of the local landowners, it preserves its territory, engages in annual release programmes, controls the major predators of game and defines a shooting regime incorporating specific shooting days (of which Sunday is almost invariably the most common) and daily bag limits. The club may also engage in habitat improvement but such activities are clearly limited by the fact that it does not own the land and has no say in the various agricultural enterprises. What makes the

club especially unique is that the members do not pay for the actual right to shoot. The annual club subscription, generally not large, incorporates an element to cover public liability and personal accident insurance. The remainder of the subscription largely goes to fund the purchase of pheasants and mallard.

Whilst some clubs, especially in the west and southwest, have the great good fortune to be blessed with more than a scattering of woodcock, the pheasant is the mainstay of the shooting of the great majority. In recent years there has been a marked increase in interest in mallard and mallard releasing.

For many years release of poults from a traditional release pen was standard practice. Results though were frequently disappointing. High predator numbers and, at best, part-time keeping combined to ensure that few released poults remained to confront the guns when the season opened on 1ˢᵗ November. As a result many clubs have moved away from summer poult release and turned instead to the release of adult birds in early spring. These adults are birds caught up on the driven shoots when the season is over. They are well-suited to the gun club scene as they have learned the gentle arts of survival since their release the previous summer. If anything, clubs would purchase more of these adult birds if they were available. However, there are not that many driven shoots in the country and demand invariably outstrips supply.

A working party from our local club gets to grips with the business of ringing the new generation of mallard before their release.

Gun clubs have an average membership of around twenty five. There is a gun club in nearly every town and village in the country, not far short of a thousand in total. Rough shooting is the usual order of the day and shooting parties typically consist of no more than two or three guns. Those clubs lucky enough to have grouse or woodcock shooting in their preserves may organise larger parties on certain days.

Like all human organisations the gun club movement is not without its share of warts and wrinkles. Some clubs are superb. They regularly engage in large scale pheasant releases, run frequent fox drives and other forms of predator control and generally provide quality shooting for the members. Other clubs are rather less than superb but can justify their existence by ensuring the availability of shooting for the people of the area. Yet other clubs are very much less than superb and do little more than collect a subscription in order to ensure that the members are adequately insured.

To the outsider, well used to paying dearly for his sport, the gun club regime must appear a most benign one. There must be precious few countries in the world where an ordinary mortal can wander so freely with dog and gun.

Benign it most certainly is but it is not without its weaknesses. Foremost of these is the fact that in many places there is no compulsion to join the local club. The club's shooting permissions are usually obtained on a word-of-mouth basis rather than tied up in some formal legal arrangement. Should a friend or neighbour of a farmer ask to shoot it is unlikely that he will be refused. As well, if such an intruder is challenged by the club, the club may very well earn the displeasure of the farmer.

It is probably true to say that the problem of non members shooting over club preserves is most pronounced in the case of clubs based upon the larger towns. With increasing urban sprawl these clubs tend to have relatively small preserves. The situation is then further exacerbated by the large number of gun owners living in the town. It is no exaggeration to suggest that there may be a hundred, or even two hundred, legally held guns in an average-sized town.

Another inherent weakness of the regime relates to the potential for commercial exploitation of game stocks. Because of the looseness of the regime, the unscrupulous, with an eye for a fast buck, have more than adequate opportunity to ply their trade. I refer here not to the properly run commercial shoots which base the sport that they provide on put-and-take species (pheasant, partridge and mallard). I refer to those who know only too well that there is a class of European 'sportsman' who will pay very large amounts of money to shoot migratory game birds which have declined considerably in their own countries. Clubs, especially in the west of Ireland, need to exercise eternal vigilance if they are to prevent the rape of their preserves.

A favoured ploy of some of these so-called 'tourist shoot promoters' is to rent a large acreage of shooting from Coillte, the State's forestry company. Having acquired a safe and legitimate haven in a forest, particularly in some of the more remote parts of the country, the promoter can bring his clients on a rampage of destruction across the preserves of neighbouring clubs. Most of these activities take place mid-week when ordinary club members are at work. It is thus extremely difficult for clubs to take effective action. Woodcock and snipe are the favoured quarry of these people.

Wherever possible clubs try to rent the shooting of forests that lie within their boundaries. This is something of a Catch-22 situation. Many of these plantations consist largely of Sitka spruce and are not exactly great havens for game, especially when the canopy closes after a few years. But if the club does not take up the letting, the danger of some entrepreneur moving in is all too real. Clubs tend to run their affairs on a fairly limited budget. Few can afford the luxury of bidding against a commercial operative who knows that he can extract a couple of hundred euros a day from each of his clients.

The 1970s and 1980s witnessed big changes in Irish agriculture. This was in direct response to joining the then-EEC. Greatly increased areas of land were sown with winter barley, a crop second-to-none for its magnetic effect upon wood pigeons, especially if there has been a significant degree of lodging. Many clubs were too slow to come to the aid of farmers when the grey hordes descended. Quickly the promoters saw an opportunity and gangs of tourist shooters became a common sight in rural Ireland as they were ferried from field to field, resplendent in their full battle fatigues. At times the level of shooting could only be described as extraordinary. Not far from where I write something akin to the Battle of the Somme broke out one July morning about a dozen years ago. The barrage continued until dusk. I watched in awe from a nearby road. There were eight gun establishments located at strategic points in a thirty acre field. Each establishment housed two gunners. Any pigeon that had the temerity to fly anywhere remotely near the field was the recipient of volley after volley until it fell or became a speck in the distant sky.

There was not a retrieving dog to be seen. Early the following morning I took our springers around the field. In minutes they picked up a half dozen pigeons that were still alive, wings broken and in some cases still bleeding. Was this sport?

In the early 1990s matters went from bad to worse. The promoters realised that they were on to a good thing and more and more 'crop protectors' were ferried to Ireland. Then something quite extraordinary happened. It became obvious that the level of summer shooting could not be justified in terms of crop protection. Prodigious bags were being taken. On one occasion a party of protectors shot 700 pigeons in a single day. So, afraid of losing their lucrative trade, the promoters went to those charged with protection of the nation's wildlife and suggested that an open season should be initiated for the wood pigeon. A clever move. Once the species acquired game bird status there could be no objections to hunting it during the appointed season.

Not wishing to upset the 'gods of tourism' the powers that be acquiesced. Unbelievably, and in total disregard for European wildlife legislation, a pigeon season was opened on 1st June and it ran to 31st January. The European Wild Bird Directive clearly states that if an open season is created for a given species it must be awarded full protection during its period of reproduction. June, July and August lie smack in the middle of the wood pigeon's breeding cycle.

Those of us who felt that the decision to open a season in mid-summer flew in the face of all that is right and sporting referred the matter to our lords and masters in Europe. Years of prevarication followed. Eventually however, the good fight was won and the open season for pigeons now runs from 1st November to 31st January.

The massive onslaught by 'tourist shooters' on the wood pigeon had two inevitable corollaries. Pigeon numbers soon began to drop and gun club members began to realise that if they did not get their collective act together farmers might not continue to be as generous with their permissions to shoot. In the cereal growing regions of the east and south, where pigeon damage to crops can be a serious issue, club members are now doing their best to provide farmers with a crop protection service. It has to be admitted though that there is still room for improvement in this area.

The good news is that the battle-clad legions are beginning to take themselves off to countries that can offer more productive shooting holidays. No doubt about it. Ireland's gain is very definitely some other country's loss.

This, then, is the background to the Irish shooting scene. Now for the birds and the shooting.

A fine bag of teal taken on a frosty night when the birds were concentrated on a part of the pool where the water was moving and unfrozen.

Of Game Birds and Seasons

To sportsmen the world over, the term 'game bird' has a broad and common meaning. It conveys an image of a creature of the chase endowed with certain characteristics. Two of these characteristics are paramount. First, the bird must be worthy quarry, fleet of wing and thus providing the hunter with a real challenge. Second, it must be very edible. No small part of the pleasure of the chase is the consumption of the fruits of one's labour.

Within these broad parameters different countries and different cultures are likely to assign their own meanings to the term. To the purist, only the aristocrats of the partridge and grouse families and, rather begrudgingly that Johnny-come-lately, the pheasant, are real game birds.

In Ireland a brave new world of conservation came into being in 1976 with the passage into law of the Wildlife Act. For the first time, with the exception of some dozen pest species, all birds received protection. Prior to this, protection was largely confined to certain quarry species during a close season (as specified in the Game Preservation Act of 1930). The 1976 act now provided for open seasons orders, at the discretion of the Minister of the day, for certain of these protected species. Such birds as appear on an annual open seasons order are thus deemed to be game birds.

The timing and duration of hunting seasons have tended to evolve over long periods of time. In a perfect world they would be directed solely by the capacity of each given species to absorb hunting pressures without detriment to its long term viability. Knowledge of such facts as the timing

ABOVE
The start of the day. Will there be a few pheasants lurking at the edge of the stubbles?

LEFT
Magpies roosting at dusk. They are one of Ireland's 'pest' species and their numbers need to be controlled if game birds are to flourish.

of the breeding cycle, the point at which the young of the year attain the size and strength of their parents, the number of weeks of undisturbed feeding that migratory species require in order to accumulate the necessary reserves to sustain them on their return journey and subsequent breeding season, and so on.

But, if for no better reason than that we live in a somewhat less than perfect world, there is more to it than that. Concepts of what is sporting and what is not can and do change. For example, not so many years ago, flapper shooting was a recognised part of the duck hunting season. Nowadays we take a jaundiced view of shooting July or August mallard whose wing feathers have not grown sufficiently to lift them from the water.

Then again there are tentacles of politics which, as the years go by, extend more and more into everyday lives. People, who have never seen a grouse, claim the right to adjudicate on our right to shoot these birds and on when we should shoot them.

As a general rule the tendency has been to remove birds from the quarry list and to reduce the length of seasons. On this issue my philosophy is simple and straightforward. We have given up enough. Unless there is very good and compelling reason to the contrary, what we have we must hold at all costs.

BELOW
The local bog, home to a variety of duck and snipe in winter.

A Wild Goose Story

A person with an interest in shooting and some passing knowledge of the geography of Ireland could be forgiven for assuming that the country must be a paradise on earth for would-be goose shooters. After all, Ireland with its wealth of shallow bays, turloughs, callows and other wetlands seems singularly well-endowed in the matter of wintering habitats. To the north west in Canada, Greenland and Iceland are the great breeding grounds of countless grey and black geese which, come autumn, wing their way across the Atlantic. Indeed, if logic could be applied to the ways of wildfowl, Ireland should be their first port of call.

Should that same person then consult the annual Open Seasons Order he would be more than a touch surprised. Indeed, if he knows his wild geese he might be tempted to believe that the author of the Open Seasons Order put pen to paper on 1st April. He would see that the greylag goose and the Canada goose are both included. So far so good. But then he would notice the extraordinary fact that the season for each of these runs from 1st September to 15th October.

I will take the greylag first. With the exception of a small number that spill across the border from long established feral flocks in Northern Ireland, and a tiny number of feral birds scattered through the rest of the country, the mid-winter population is composed of migrants. Few of these have reached our shore by mid-October. See what I mean about 1st April?

ABOVE
The geese that don't like Ireland. A skein of pinkfoot geese over Scottish stubbles.

13

The reality is that there is a six week season but, effectively, there are no geese to shoot.

The story of Canada goose is not that different. There are hardly any of them in the Republic. Most of those that are here have come, like the feral greylags, from across the border. Counties Leitrim and Monaghan are faring best as the overspill has resulted in small breeding populations in these counties. Elsewhere, with the exception of a couple of localised spots in County Cork, the chances of seeing a Canada goose are negligible. More on the Canada goose later.

Readers who delve into later chapters of this book will find no further mention of wild geese. Clearly an explanation is necessary, so here are some facts and figures to set the ball rolling. Five main species of wild geese are found in Ireland during the winter months: three of these are black geese and two are grey. In total they number some 50,000 birds, probably less than the number of pinkfeet wintering in Aberdeenshire.

The shooting of migratory black geese ceased in Ireland many years ago. The Barnacle has never come in large numbers and is mainly confined to the islands off the north and west coasts. They are part of a population that breeds in Greenland. About 8,000 come to Ireland. The greater part of that breeding population passes on to the western coast of Scotland.

In the case of the smaller Brent there is no real reason why it could not be hunted. Its removal from the quarry list had little to do with conservation requirements and a lot to do with politics. In the 1930s the dark bellied race of this species which breeds in arctic Russia and Siberia and winters in Britain went into serious decline. This was attributed to the disappearance of the marine grass, Zostera, its main food plant.

Forbidden fruit, a skein of Brent geese overhead, and no more than 30 yards up!

Because of the decline, Brent goose shooting in Britain was stopped.

Ireland fell in line with this decision even though the dark-bellied Brent does not grace our shores. There was absolutely no need to stop Brent goose shooting here. Our wintering birds are of the pale-bellied race which breed in arctic Canada. Unlike its dark-bellied counterpart, it was never in decline. To the present day it has maintained its numbers and in an average winter there are in excess of 20,000 scattered on suitable sites around the coast. If anything, the pale-bellied Brent is now better established than ever before. This is due in no small measure to dietary change. First observed in County Wexford in the 1970s, the Brent has taken a liking to pasture fields and young crops of winter cereals. Such an enhanced diet sets it up well for the long flight back to Canada and the ensuing breeding season.

As every shooting man knows, persuading officialdom to return a species to the hunting list once it has been removed is something akin to banging one's head against a brick wall. It requires fervour, it requires passion and it requires a stomach for the long haul. The first priority is a real desire on the part of the majority to get the bird returned. To be frank I doubt that such desire now exists. The Brent has become a rather tame little goose though I suspect that a few well-directed volleys could cause it to seriously review its relationship with mankind. Then there is the matter of its flesh. In time past few people regarded the Brent goose as a real gastronomic experience. A diet of marine vegetation tends to produce meat that is best described as tough and oily. It may well be that a Brent goose that has spent a few weeks feeding inland could have more culinary appeal. By analogy a wigeon shot over a flooded water meadow provides a much more pleasing meal than its cousin shot over mudflats.

A handful of genuinely wild Canada geese turn up in Ireland in most winters. They are migrants from the other side of the Atlantic who probably got caught up with a flight of white-fronts and so ended up in County Wexford instead of their intended destination along the fringes of the Bay of Mexico.

Canada geese appear to have been brought to England during the reign of Charles II (1660–1685). But, like many introduced species, they took a long time to settle and it was much later – probably well into the 19th century – that some of these birds were brought to Ireland.

When a creature is uprooted and deposited in totally new surroundings it is recognised that, if its kind are to survive the transplant, it must undergo a period of adaptation to equip it for life in the new country. During this quiescent period slow and subtle genetic selection takes place. Quiescent periods tend to be long rather than short. By 1953, nearly 300 years after the initial introductions, a census in Britain found only 6,000 birds. But then, less than 50 years on, it would appear that the right genes were finally in place as the population exploded to pest proportions.

In Ireland the story to date is very different. There are presently no more than 1,000 birds in the entire country. The great majority of these are in Northern Ireland. Three points can, I think, be made. The first is the most obvious. Canada geese have only been in Ireland for some 150 years and will probably require a lot more time to adapt to the prevailing conditions. This assumes that it will be able to adapt, for such is never a foregone conclusion.

The second point concerns habitat. The enormous expansion in motorway construction and other building programmes that took place in England in the 1950s, particularly in the south east, left in its wake an abundance of worked-out gravel pits. Very many of these were flooded and adapted to the needs of waterfowl. Part of that process of developing the worked-out pits involved the creation of islands. Undoubtedly the Canada goose benefited, especially as a result of secure nesting sites becoming available on these islands. Ireland, with its much smaller human population is unlikely to see gravel diggings of this scale. In consequence suitable breeding habitat may be, I suspect, insufficient to meet the needs of an expanding population.

The third point is that, bearing in mind the shooting regime which operates across the Republic, it is going to be very difficult for the goose to expand its range. With no intended disrespect to my fellow sportsmen, should a large and alien goose appear overhead in the course of a day's rough shooting it might, just might, even with the most Christian and law-abiding of men, prove to be an irresistible temptation.

Some years ago I acquired three pairs of Canada geese and released them on a twenty acre lake in the grounds of a nearby boarding school. The lake is studded with islands and is a wildfowl sanctuary. I expected great things but alas it was not to be. Everyone insisted on feeding the geese with the result that they became incredibly tame. Their appetites were insatiable and they soon found the row of dustbins outside the school kitchens. It was all downhill after that. On a daily basis the bins were turned upside down as my geese scavenged without fear. Tolerance thresholds quickly dropped and it was decided that they had to go. End of experiment.

Now for the grey geese, for these are what goose shooting in these islands is really all about.

We will start with that most extraordinary anomaly. Each autumn Scotland and eastern England play host to countless thousands of pinkfeet. These have come from Greenland and Iceland. I have often crouched low at the edge of a stubble field in eastern Scotland of an October morning and watched in sheer amazement as flight after flight of the baying packs swing in to feed. I doubt that as many as a dozen come to Ireland. I have never seen one in Ireland. What have we done wrong? We have the barley stubbles, we have suitable bays and sea loughs on which they could roost. It is just not fair.

Fifty years ago two species of grey geese, the greylag and the white-front were widespread in Ireland. The former probably had bred for centuries on the great central and western bogs. Each autumn its numbers were augmented by a plentiful supply of migrants from Iceland. Some areas played host to very large numbers. On the Wexford Slobs for example, two polders lying to the north and south of Wexford harbour which had been reclaimed from the sea in the 19th century, up to 10,000 greylags were spotted in some winters up until 1945.

Thereafter, without apparent reason, greylag numbers plummeted across the country and two decades later there were less than one thousand to be found in Ireland. 1967 marked the lowest point. Yet another species was lost from the quarry list.

There has never been a really satisfactory explanation as to why the greylag deserted Ireland. Certainly one cannot point to any great change in environment or agricultural regime during that era. It is known that during those years of decline wintering numbers enlarged significantly in Scotland. To some extent Scotland's gain must have been Ireland's loss.

One suggestion put forward was that the big expansion that took place in tillage farming in Scotland during the post war years provided a lot of safe and attractive new feeding sites – more attractive than those available in Ireland.

Whatever the reason for the decline there is a modicum of hope for the goose-starved Irish shooter. Greylag numbers are at last building again and are presently reaching around 6,000 by December. The $64,000 question is at what population level will a proper winter season be reintroduced? We are talking some years into the future and, judging from past history, there will be a long and acrimonious battle to be fought before the greylag can again be shot in winter.

Finally there is that most Irish and most sought-after of all the wild geese, the white-front. In 1948 the late Peter Scott recognised that the white-front found in Ireland was somewhat different from the one wintering in England. In particular it had an orange bill rather than a pink one. These Irish birds are of a separate race which breeds in Greenland. In addition to Ireland they winter along the western fringes of Scotland.

The traditional haunts of the white-front in Ireland were the bogs of the central and western counties. It appears that they were never very numerous in Munster. In the mid-1920s they made their first appearance on the Wexford Slobs and within a decade numbers there were steadily increasing. It would seem that fairly short-cropped pasture fields of the Slobs provided more attractive feeding than the rough grasses of the western bogs. Numbers in Wexford continued to increase and with the departure of the greylags in the 1960s, the white-fronts became the main geese of the Slobs. For several decades somewhere around 7,000 could be counted each winter. During those years a number of medium-sized flocks and many small ones remained faithful to their bogland habitat. In Scotland the single biggest flock was, and still is, found on the Isle of Islay.

In the late 1970s claims began to emanate from the small but vociferous bird watching community that white-front numbers were declining. Despite a lack of any real evidence to support this contention, officialdom took it seriously. But then that is forever the way. The bird watchers are always the good guys and the shooters are always the bad guys. In the mindset of officialdom you cannot have regard for birds if you shoot them. And this despite the fact that the shooting fraternity does far more in Ireland than any other group to provide for the needs of birds.

Pressures mounted and in 1982 the last wild goose was struck from the Open Seasons Order. After centuries, goose shooting in Ireland was at an end. A four year 'moratorium' was declared but, it was stated, white-front shooting would be restored unless incontrovertible evidence necessitated a continuation of the moratorium. That incontrovertible evidence was never forthcoming. Despite this, and with the exception of two short seasons confined to the county of Wexford, the moratorium has continued to the present day.

Battle was joined in earnest and goose shooters were subjected to a quite extraordinary level of duplicity for more than a decade. Goal posts rarely stayed in the same place for long. As soon as one of officialdom's arguments had been put to the sword another quickly replaced it.

Meanwhile, in Iceland, where the white-fronts stop over for a few short weeks in September and early October on their way from Greenland, shooting continued. And it continues to the present day.

Finally, in the early 1990s we were told that a conference of the range states i.e. Greenland, Iceland, Ireland and Britain would take place in Wexford. As part of its deliberations, we were assured, the question of shooting would be fully addressed and quotas agreed for countries with wintering populations. The conference took place but Iceland did not bother to attend. Not to worry; they would be contacted and the matter would be resolved, so said officialdom. Another decade has passed and nothing has happened. Goose shooters have grown weary of the fight.

One last comment and I will write no more of the wild geese. At the beginning of this chapter I outlined the weird and wonderful goose seasons that appear on the Open Seasons Order. There is only one reason why the greylag and the Canada grace the Open Seasons Order. They are there to create the illusion that goose shooting has returned. And that is all it is – an illusion.

Waiting for the Season to Open

Game hunting is an addiction, of that there is little doubt. It is an addiction from which I am happy to suffer and one for which I will apologise to no man. It is an addiction with origins buried deep in primeval caverns of the human psyche. It is an addiction which stems directly from a genetic programme of prehistoric man which ensured the survival of our kind. That programme was brief and to the point. Kill or starve.

The basic thesis of those who oppose hunting is that, since we no longer need to hunt for food, we should no longer do so. They then invariably prattle on about cruelty, sentient beings and the rights of animals. My answer to them is this. The god who made us all, hunter and anti alike, created an order of things in which, since animal life appeared on earth, required the killing of one organism by another. There is no reason why the passage of time should necessitate an alteration to this divinely inspired order of things.

Anyway, enough about antis. If they want to appear in print they can write their own books.

One great problem with addictions is the sheer pain of severance. As an ex-smoker I know only too well of the agony endured when one forsakes the evil weed. But at least it is a one-off. After some weeks the pain begins to lessen and then finally it disappears.

With game shooting it is a rather different matter. The pain of severance is an annual one. On 31st January I am free to hunt snipe, teal,

ABOVE
The gate was jammed and, yes, the gun is broken.

LEFT
The best of companions for flighting in the darkness. Without my springer many a bird would be impossible to gather up at this time in the day.

19

woodcock or other such species as my fancy dictates. Next day I cannot do so. Then there are seven long months before I can pander to my addiction once more.

That is not to say that there is nothing to do during the close season. The luckiest man, in my estimation, is he who draws as much satisfaction from fishing as he does from shooting. For him only a few short weeks intervene before he can indulge himself in the pursuit of trout and salmon. Here the citizens of Ireland are extremely fortunate. Most of us live near a river or lake that can be fished for brown trout. In many cases permission to fish is readily obtainable from the landowner. Alternatively it is not an inordinately expensive matter to join a club which owns or rents fishing rights.

Ireland has a lot of what are called derelict fisheries. My understanding of this term is that they are fisheries for which there is no recorded owner or ones for which the rights have not been exercised for many years. As was the case with game rights, I suspect that a lot of fishing rights 'got lost' because of the vagaries of some of the Land Acts.

I would dearly love to achieve the same degree of satisfaction from fishing as I do from shooting. Alas, that is not the case and I truly envy those who do. Certainly there is a 'buzz' when the line suddenly tightens and a pound of fighting fury tries all in its power to escape. Space and time become suspended until the fury is tamed and the fish is safely on the bank. Some people then admire it and put it back. I do not. I caught it in order that I and my family could eat it.

Fly fishing, which is the only branch of fishing about which I feel vaguely qualified to write, comes basically in two forms. Experts, with a skill born of years, fish the dry fly. Ordinary mortals like me settle for the wet fly. I will only comment on the wet fly. Biologically one is trying to tempt the trout by using a replica of some larval insect or nymph. Countless patterns and colours have been developed which, according to the time of year, provide irresistible temptation. At least that is the theory.

ABOVE
The Golden Vale
from the Vee Gap in
the Knockmealdown
mountains. The Galtee
mountains can be seen in
the distance.

LEFT
The River Suir in spate
from Ardfinnan Bridge in
County Tipperary.

I grew up in an era in which fishing was a late evening event. This for no better reason than the demands of farming were such as to require the attention of men until the day was well and truly ended. Around eight or nine of a summer's evening we would check that the flies from the previous evening were not too tattered and take the short walk across the field to the river. Expert fishermen know exactly which flies to use. After the early season March Browns, Iron Blue Duns and Olives, we used the same three flies for the rest of the summer. Many years later I still use the same three patterns. And, I have to admit, immodestly, with similar success. In the late 1960s a brother-in-law and I once caught forty six trout of a July evening.

In pride of place at the end of the cast was the Gold Rail, in my estimation the greatest killer of them all. If, due to the incompetence of the owner of the local hardware store, where we purchased our flies, the Gold Rail was not available, Wyckham's Fancy was not too bad a substitute. Some eighteen inches back on the first dropper was the Silver Rail. On its night it could prove its worth. Occasionally it killed when the Gold Rail did not but more often than not it had to settle for second best. The second dropper always carried a Bloody Butcher. More on that fly later.

The best trout streams as far as I am concerned alternate between shallow, fast water bursting and bubbling over protruding rocks and slow, deep stretches. For reasons that I cannot explain trout will take the wet fly in fast water long before they deign to feed in the deeper water. In the hour which ends in dusk I always fish the shallows. The current quickly

carries my three flies to the end of the fast water. Not infrequently some small and badly educated two ounce fish gets hooked. Should this not happen I move the triumvirate slowly back towards me. The junction of fast and slow water is, at this time of evening, a great killing point. I think that the trout take up position there for two reasons. The rapid flow is such as to propel a stream of well-oxygenated water across their gills. It also carries down plenty of morsels of tasty insect life. Many of the finest trout that I have caught before the light has left the western sky have surrendered at that junction between fast and slow water.

As darkness falls, and this may be well after 11pm in early July, the rise fades away in the shallows. Time now to move to still, dark brooding waters, preferably where alder and willow overhang. The light has all but gone but a satisfactory 'plop' and a just-visible circular ripple bear witness to the fact that tomorrow's breakfast is willing to make the supreme sacrifice. This is where the Bloody Butcher comes into its own. The biggest and best trout that I have caught have succumbed to its charms. The combination of dark blue, silver and red seems irresistible in the still, dark night. I have no doubt that the strand of silver provides the icing on the cake. Down the years when, once again the same local hardware owner's incompetence has meant that I could not get a Bloody Butcher, I have tried his cousin, the Scarlet Butcher. It is much the same as the Bloody Butcher but without the silver and with rather more red. I do not think that I have ever caught a trout with this apology for a fly. I have tried and I have tried again. I am convinced beyond all reasonable doubt that the trout of Tipperary have nothing but the utmost contempt for the Scarlet Butcher.

There is little more that I can say about fishing. I enjoy the sultry evenings on the banks of the Suir and its tributaries. But I must be honest. I would not swap one winter's evening, when the Suir has burst its banks and the cock wigeon are whistling in the darkening sky, for a week of sultry July nights. This is not to decry the pleasures of angling but we are creatures of our genes. Each to his own. I was born a shooter. Others are born fishermen. Those lucky few upon whom the Gods have undoubtedly smiled, are equally happy as shooters in the winter and fishermen in the summer.

There are plenty of other things to do in the long months that separate January from September. Many of these, whilst not of the stuff of adrenaline secretion, are vital to our sport. Predator control is clearly one of these. Indeed, Ireland, without the level of gamekeeping which is the norm elsewhere, has far too many enemies of game. Four in particular need dedicated and ongoing attention. They are the fox and the magpie, the grey-back and the mink.

The fox population is enormous and, in my experience, expanding at a quite alarming rate. Less than thirty years ago between one and two percent of the country was planted with trees. Today it is about ten percent. The massive increase in afforestation has provided the fox with a superabundance of secure cover, especially in the impenetrable depths of young spruce plantations. From these safe havens they can make nightly journeys of depredation, covering maybe thirty or forty kilometres. They will then return to their dens long before the first streaks of dawn cross the eastern sky.

Most people, and this includes shooting people who spend a lot of time in wild and lonesome places, only occasionally encounter foxes. But once in a while one receives a forcible reminder of just how many of them there really are. The morning after a fall of snow usually tells its own eloquent story. The neat pointed paw prints are literally everywhere in the fields. And that simple message is heavily underlined should the snow lie for a few days.

I spend quite a lot of time walking the mountains. Only on a handful of occasions, despite the proximity of plantations, can I recall meeting a fox in the uplands. One early September morning, though, I parked the car in what long ago had been a farmyard at the mountain's edge. The surrounding vegetation was high and almost impenetrable. But an overgrown path provided access to the mountain. As grouse are apt to spring from the most unlikely places, I had already loaded my gun. Not a hundred yards from where I had left the car the path veered sharply to the left. As I took this turn sheer pandemonium erupted. Foxes that had been feasting on the carcass of a mountain sheep fled in all directions. I shot two with ease and at least half a dozen more disappeared into the heather.

We rely upon two main strategies for fox shooting: driving and lamping. Both are effective but of their very nature require great care. In theory a fox drive is a simple operation. Guns go to appointed positions

at the end and sides of the cover and the beaters then move forward accompanied by two or three springers. The vital thing is that everyone knows the plan of campaign and is aware of where everyone else is positioned. A back gun is always a good idea as foxes are adept at creeping backwards through the beating line. On numerous occasions when walking a field of beet for pheasants I have seen Reynard, belly literally dragging the ground, sneaking back between the drills.

Lamping foxes is a legitimate exercise in Ireland as long as the landowner's consent has been obtained. A black, windy night between moons is ideal; the colder and hungrier the better. A team of two is ideal, the lamp man and the shooter. If the lamp man is proficient at imitating a squealing rabbit, so much the better. I have lamped foxes with

some real artists. Such was their calling skill that the fox would come running into the beam.

Electronic calls are now readily available but I do not think that I really approve of them. Maybe I am old-fashioned but they give me a sense of cheating. I believe that there are certain areas of life from which modern technology should be excluded. The hunting field is one of these.

Foxes are fast learners so it is imperative that once the lamp picks up that pair of red eyes the shot finds its mark. In my experience a fox that has survived such an operation is not going to be caught easily a second time. A sure sign of a lamp-shy fox is its rapid disappearance through a ditch the moment the spotlight falls on it.

Magpies require continuous and urgent attention. There are far too many of them in Ireland and they have few equals in the bird world when it comes to successfully rearing a large brood. Our mild springs result in early breeding and the big domed nests are clearly visible long before the foliage has emerged. By May the excited chattering of the parents is a sure sign that they are trying to lead the family out of harm's way.

Surprisingly, the magpie is not a native Irish bird. It is believed that is first appeared in the country in 1676. Following a ferocious storm a flock was observed in Wexford, presumably having been blown across from Wales. It must have been some storm. Whatever about its origins, the magpie quickly decided that Ireland was very much to its liking. Town and country were colonized with equal zeal. There can be no capital city in the world with a bigger magpie population than that of Dublin. At the present day it is estimated that there are between 650,000 and 700,000

LEFT
A moment's respite for the author before the serious flames erupt from the heather.

BELOW
The heather is nicely ablaze and under control: time for a well-earned rest. Note the snow lying less than 50 yards above us.

of them in the country. An early morning car journey provides revealing insight into the sheer number of magpies. Literally every squashed rabbit carcass has two or more of these black and white marauders dancing in attendance.

Few will argue with the contention that the Larsen trap reigns supreme in the matter of magpie control. Properly sited I have seen traps deliver up two captives morning after morning. A Larsen trap will catch in all seasons but I find that the greatest success is to be had in late autumn and early summer. In late autumn magpies gather in communal roosts. The sheer numbers present (there can be twenty or more) all but guarantees rich pickings. By June, unless very careful attention has been paid to all the nests in the area, families of young magpies are ripe for the taking.

Shooting has a place in magpie control but the opportunities are limited. They are jittery birds and have a sneaky habit of slipping away on the far side of the ditch. Best to locate the nests and then wait until incubation is well underway. The cock bird is usually not too far away and he will do all in his power to call his mate away at the first sight of humanity. Only when she is really broody will she be inclined to disregard his summons. Then is the time to approach the nest, a gun at each side. The resulting shot can be a testing one. On emerging from the nest a magpie will frequently dip sharply and beat the best of shots. I always wait until her flight straightens out and she is departing low across the field.

The grey-back or scald crow, as the hooded crow is know in Ireland, is the second of the corvids to require regular attention. It cannot match the magpie's efficiency as an egg thief but is capable of causing serious damage in the early part of the year before cover for ground nesters has developed sufficiently. Mallard are especially prone to the crow's depredations at this time. They are very early nesters and it is not unusual for the clutch to be completed well

before the end of March. Grey-backs have a particular liking for young ducklings as well as eggs. I have witnessed a pair swooping down and plucking the ducklings from the water. They returned again and again until the brood was decimated.

The Larsen trap is also very effective against grey-backs. Some people favour the side entry version for crows but I find the top entry one that we use for magpies just as efficient.

Like magpies, grey-backs can be shot at the nest. Once again it is best to wait until they have become unwilling to leave the eggs. The late evening is a good time to carry out the assassination as they seem to become a little less wary as the light fades.

Roost shooting provides a good opportunity to make serious inroads into a local population. These normally solitary birds frequently gather in large numbers at a communal roost of a winter's evening. The secret is to be in a well-concealed position sometime before the flight begins. High elm ditches used to be favoured roosts. Now, following the elm's demise courtesy of Dutch Elm Disease, ivy-shrouded oaks or ashes are mainly used. You only get one opportunity so the more guns the better. Once the barrage has started the survivors will make several attempts to return. Some will try to slip in when it is almost completely dark. If you go back next evening you will almost certainly find that the place has been deserted.

THE PROBLEM OF MINK

The story of mink in Ireland began about fifty years ago. Small farmers, mainly in the border counties, were looking for new enterprises to boost their incomes in an era of depressed agricultural prices. They were extremely badly advised to consider mink. Within a few years fifty or sixty mink farms were in operation. It was not long before escapes occurred and it was not long before the owners began to realise that mink eat an awful lot of meat and take a long time to produce a return. In some cases, realising that they had backed a loser, the owners simply opened the gates and let off the inmates.

Ireland is well-endowed with waterways and these mink soon spread across the country. In a few short years there was a thriving feral population. Mink are now well-established in every county. There is no doubt in my mind that numbers are steadily expanding. Unbelievably, when the threat to fish and fowl became apparent, we were told not to worry. Mink, said the experts, are highly territorial and once territories have been established, the population will level off. My every experience is the contrary. No more than a couple of miles from here is the river Suir, arguably the finest brown trout river in these inlands. One March not too many years ago I asked a farmer whose land adjoins the river if he would operate a trap for me. We decided upon a location where numerous star-shaped footprints at a sandy edge indicated a coming-ashore venue. Before that month of March had ended he had accounted

LEFT
A magpie nest – to be approached quietly, ideally with a gun either side of the bush.

27

for eleven mink at this one spot. Territory? Gun clubs on other stretches of the Suir have had similar experiences.

In theory mink can be controlled. Extermination though is not a starter. By now they are too well-established in the wild. The cage trap is deadly. Having experimented with fresh fish, tinned fish, beef, lamb, dog food and every other conceivable form of animal protein, I am firmly of the view that a fresh hind leg of a rabbit is the best bait. The problem is finding time to regularly visit the trap. The best trapping sites are often remote and demand a stiff hike from the car. One can do it for a couple of weeks but it is really an operation that should be ongoing. For this reason I am more than a little pessimistic about the mink situation. I feel that they will forever pose a serious threat to Irish wildlife.

Other than predator control there are two shooting-related activities from which I get a lot of satisfaction during the close season. They are very different. One is heather burning. The other is releasing and minding mallard on our flight ponds. Before passing on to these I should, I suppose, comment on the fact that I have used the term predator control rather than vermin control. I suspect that I am just engaging in political correctness. Those predators are vermin and there is no good reason for calling them anything else.

Now for heather burning. To state that one enjoys burning things puts one in danger of being thought of as a pyromaniac. I assure you that this is not the case. Though, it has to be admitted, the adrenaline levels do tend to go through the ceiling when, as is often the case, the fire looks as if it is getting out of control. More on that later.

As every grouse-lover knows, the fate of the bird is inextricably tied to the age and quality of the heather. Few species can be more dependant upon a single plant. Other than when it is a chick, and like all young birds requires the high protein content of insect bodies to propel it at knots to maturity, the grouse needs heather. According to season it consumes the shoots, leaves, flowers and seeds. Heather growth of the first three years in the most nutritious. But the demands of grouse extend beyond the requirement for high quality heather. They must also have higher and older growth in which to hide and rest. Moreover, they want it in close proximity to their food. No self respecting grouse will feed far from cover. There is always the possibility that the shadow of a peregrine or a harrier will cross the moor and they want to be able to slip quietly and discreetly out of sight. In consequence the art of grouse management has long centred around selective burning designed to produce a mix of heather plants of different ages.

ABOVE
Fresh grouse droppings,
always a welcome sight
to revive the flagging
spirits during a long day
on the hill.

LEFT
Time to deal with a
successful Larsen trap
catch. Once re-set, more
magpies may well come
to it later in the day.

For many years Irish grouse could be considered both lucky and unlucky. This seems like a contradiction. I will explain. Until comparatively recently mountain sheep farming was a flourishing business aided as it was by subsidies from Europe. If anything there were parts of the country in which it flourished too well. An excess of sheep appeared on the hills and their sheer numbers resulted in serious degradation of the heather. I know of places where the heather disappeared altogether and to date has not returned.

Mountain sheep thrive on young heather. For this reason the mountain shepherds burned high ground every year to ensure a good supply. Because of this the grouse shooters were lucky. There was no need for them to burn the heather themselves.

Unfortunately the shepherd's objective was not quite at one with that of the grouse shooter. The shepherd wanted endless acres of young growth upon which his lambs could grow fat. The grouse preserver wanted a patchwork.

Most years things worked out quite well. Because of the vagaries of the weather, especially in mountainous regions, burning was rarely too extensive. Either the rain would come or the underlying peat would be too damp for the heather to really take off. Maybe the burned patches were bigger than we would have really liked but they were infinitely preferable to a sea of old, rank heather.

This being said there was the occasional disaster year. Because of the difficulty of getting a fire to take off in a damp spring, and contrary to wildlife legislation, it was not unknown for a lighted match to fall into bone dry heather in May or June. The resulting conflagration could blaze for days and result in a stretch of burned ground extending over a number of miles. Two years later it would look quite superb in summer, an endless vista of purple. But of absolutely no use to grouse.

Times have changed mightily. And they have changed with unnerving speed. The mountain sheep is now on the brink of becoming an endangered species. And with its decline the traditional practice of heather burning has effectively ground to a halt. It was not too long before the effect on grouse habitat became apparent. Good quality heather-feeding grew scarcer and scarcer.

We were left with no option. If our sport was not to die, heather burning would just have to become a regular feature on the calendar. And so it has. It is never an easy operation for there are a number of problems. The first of these concerns the time of year when it is permissible to burn vegetation on uncultivated ground. We are confined to the period starting on 1st September and ending the last day of February. The autumn can be discounted for the very simple reason that the shooting season is in progress and it would be no more than wishful thinking to expect to get the troops out when they could be more profitably employed in the pursuit of game. That means that we are effectively confined to the month of February. And then, since most of us have to go out to earn a living, we are further confined to weekends. It therefore becomes necessary to watch the weather forecasts avidly and pray for good weather. In fact February is usually a good month and we usually succeed in getting a few suitable days.

At high altitude, we mainly operate above 1200 feet, the wind is usually brisk and the heather can be surprisingly dry after a couple of days without rain. The turf and underlying mosses however are likely to be a little on the damp side. This is not a major problem. Indeed it can be advantageous as it reduces the risk of the flames spreading madly out of control.

The second problem that we face relates to the nature of the terrain. Burning heather high up in the mountains is a very different proposition

Waiting for the fire to extinguish itself. Extreme vigilance is always necessary in the vicinity of plantations.

to carrying out the same task on a flat, lowland moor. To compound the problem there are conifer plantations all around at lower level. We would hardly endear ourselves to the foresters if they went up in flames.

For safety's sake, and to do a decent job, one needs a lot of bodies. A minimum of around a dozen is advisable. What we try to do first is burn a fire-break some few hundred yards down-wind. I say 'try' because the eddying of the wind frequently prevents the translation of theory into practice. If the manoeuvre is successful it is then a matter of retreating and burning strips towards the break. We try to keep the strips about twenty or thirty yards in width and one hundred yards apart. Again one is very much at the mercy of the wind. Not infrequently strips become patches of irregular shape. This does not matter in the least. The basic objective is to promote new growth. Everything else is secondary.

An essential item of equipment is some implement to beat out the flames. A farmyard shovel will suffice but it is heavy and clumsy and unsuited to a long day. Best of all are the wooden handles with a large rubber flap attached. In the right hands they are very effective. We operate by having a couple of men following the fire on either side of the strip. Their main role is to stop the strip expanding.

With the best will in the world matters can get out of hand. A sudden gust of wind just as the flames engulf a particular high and dense patch of heather can have a dramatic effect. Suddenly the flames are leaping for the sky and there is a positive roar from the burning vegetation. Now is the time for steady nerves. Try to keep ahead of the fire, sometimes easier said than done on account of the great heat, and channel the two sides of the strip into a point.

Starting a fire is not always easy. In the early days we humped straw, diesel oil, old tyres, paper and other combustibles up the hill. Sometimes it worked, sometimes it did not. Then we found the answer: a gas torch which is easily connected to a small cylinder. A picnic-size cylinder, we discovered, was more than sufficient to ensure a full day's burning. The blow torch has never let us down.

A day's heather burning is an arduous occupation, let there be no doubt of that. We are talking of seven or eight hours' slog over rough and uneven terrain. Then there is the temperature. Before operations begin it may well be close to zero at that time of year. On two occasions this February there was snow lying less than one hundred feet above where we were burning. If the wind is in the east or north, as is often the case at this time of year, the wind-chill factor can be quite severe. One minute one is perished, the next the heather is ablaze and it is necessary to retreat from the heat. A man needs to be in the prime of his health to absorb such temperature fluctuations over a long day.

When evening finally falls there is a feeling of great elation. Weary and soot-stained we can survey numerous burned patches which are evidence of a job well done. These patches are likely to be spread over many hundred acres of the mountain. All that is left is the long walk back to the cars, mere specks in the valley beneath. Then it is time for a few, or perhaps more than a few, pints of the black stuff to restore the flagging spirits. Next week, given fair weather, we will be back for more.

Releasing mallard is an exercise from which I derive enormous satisfaction. Unlike young pheasants, which can be fragile and difficult creatures to manage, they are a pleasure to handle. Ducklings are tough and resilient and there is always a good chance of bringing an entire batch to the stage at which they are airborne. That can rarely be said of pheasants. In engineering that transition from semi-domestic bird to wild bird, there is one basic imperative. The release site must be such as to ensure safety from predators, to the greatest possible degree, until the young mallard have learned the ways of an evil world. This objective is most easily achieved by releasing on a pond with one or more islands.

Some people use a release pen that runs down into the water. After a few days of acclimatisation, one end is opened and the young ducks are given their freedom of the pond. If the pen can be constructed on an island, so much the better. I have come to the conclusion however that a pen is not necessary as long as the ducklings have reached a certain stage of maturity when they are put on the water. This means a minimum age of six or seven weeks. The structure of the island is important. The bigger it is the better. A lot of vegetation is highly desirable as it provides facilities for scavenging and, at least in the early stages, reduces the temptation to wander on the surrounding land.

The island should also have broad and gently sloping banks upon which the young birds can loaf and roost. They are also an excellent place for feeding. The release battle is more than half won if one can encourage one's charges to roost on the island.

FEEDING ROUTINES FOR YOUNG MALLARD

For this reason I feed twice a day during the immediate post-release period. A couple of hundred yards from our main pond is a pump house that served a now long-disused well. In this I keep a supply of food and an old pair of waders. It is right at the back of the farm but the long trudge in the early morning and late evening is well worthwhile if the feeding regime succeeds in educating the ducks properly. I leave the evening feed until it is all but dusk. There are two reasons for this. I work on the theory that, having been well fed, the birds will stay on the island for the night. In most cases they tend to do so. Then there is the matter of foxes. This is the hour when they emerge from their dens and set out on the prowl. It is a good time to persuade them to give the pond a wide berth. Human activity is a good deterrent and I make a point of making as much noise as possible as I go abut my chores. For good measure I bring the gun with me and fire two or three shots before leaving.

More professional duck releasers than I may regard such methodology as verging on the primitive. So be it. All that I can say is that it works for me and most years we have no more than a handful of losses before the shooting season.

In all release programmes the level and type of feeding is critical. It is really a balancing act between, on the one hand, providing sufficient food of sufficient quality to maximise growth rates and stop the birds from straying and, on the other hand, not overdoing it and producing fat, tame ducks which prefer to waddle rather than fly. It is all too easy to start off with a proprietary brand of pellets and them move on to an exclusive diet of grain. I am less than convinced that this is the best procedure for mallard. In the wild their diet is wide and varied. I believe that the sooner one can get them eating a range of different foods the better. For no better reason than sheer convenience we make barley or wheat the bulk constituent of their feed. But we add as many different items as possible. Until a few years ago we grew seven or eight acres of potatoes and there was always plenty of small and misformed ones available. Chopping them up was a bit of a chore but the ducks certainly thrived on them. Turnip and carrot tops and peelings, cabbage, bad apples and household scraps are all received with enthusiasm.

Once the ducks start to take their first tentative flights we scale back the feeding to once per day. Then, with the passage of time, the odd day is omitted in an attempt to reduce over-dependency. At this time of year barley stubbles are appearing and they soon learn to fly out and forage. Once the shooting season comes in we further reduce the feeding to every second or third day. Ideally, by now, they have grown quite wild and rise in unison at human approach.

Getting released mallard to fly can be a simple matter one year and a thorough pain the next. Once they are able to skitter along the surface we introduce them to our springers. These liver and white and black and white bundles of non-stop activity have learned their trade chasing woodcock out of the most impenetrable of cover. They will not tolerate any bird sitting on land or water. At first we only use one. Until the ducks have received a modicum of primary education, two dogs are liable to execute a pincer movement with potentially disastrous consequences for the victim. The first time that the ducks meet a dog their response is best described as one of incredulity. Suddenly, instead of the benign beings to whom they have become accustomed, a thoroughly obnoxious and malignant creature has entered their universe. They leap from the water, fly a few yards and scatter in all directions. The circus continues

This feeding raft, netted to deter pigeons and other free-loaders, provides the young mallard with plentiful corn in the weeks following their release. They will return to feed regularly as long as corn supplies last.

until the malignant canine presence, after a summer of virtual inactivity, comes out of the pond shattered, sits down and sulks. A few more similar lessons, then the advanced course with a couple of springers can commence. Finally graduation day arrives and the class pass out with honours. At the very appearance of the dogs the entire population of the pond takes to the air with a roar of wings and assorted quackings. Job done. All that remains is to keep feeding the pond at the minimum level required to keep the inhabitants happy.

Sometimes the duck farm includes an albino or two in our order. We normally take little heed of them and they simply have to take their chances like the rest. But last year there was one for which I developed a special affection. It was the best flyer of the lot and a born leader. Once the batch were flying well the white duck was invariably the first to leap from the pond when disturbed. When stubble visitations were underway in July it could be seen leading its formation back and forth.

One afternoon in August I was working near the pond and the ducks were coming and going as is their wont as this time of year. I happened to look up just as a flight of some dozen birds came in high over the grove. They were intent on landing on the pond but on seeing me, veered away. I turned back to whatever I was doing only to hear a rush of wings in very close proximity. Simultaneously I was conscious of a rush of air across the side of my face. The white mallard was passing over my shoulder at speed no more than three or four feet away. Just behind him and almost in striking range was a peregrine falcon. I suspect that it was so intent on catching the duck that it had failed to notice me initially. On seeing me it banked sharply and then flapped away in leisurely fashion seemingly unconcerned at the loss of a snack. The mallard, meanwhile, swept down and landed on the water. I walked over to a point about fifty yards from the pond to see if there would be a chapter two. Despite my presence the mallard made no attempt to rise as it would normally have done. Instead it swam slowly into the bank at a point where a clump of rushes overhang the water. There it sat motionless uttering an occasional low pitched little quack. It was clearly highly traumatized. After about ten minutes I walked over to the pond to see what it would do. It made no attempt to fly away. Next morning normal service resumed. At my approach the white mallard led his colleagues away as usual.

Because of that moment of destiny I decided that this bird had earned a little special treatment. Orders were issued; it was not to be shot. Orders were obeyed and it stayed with us until shortly before Christmas. Then, when the water meadows filled along the Suir, our duck, as is their wont, started to visit them. One day the white duck failed to return with others. We never saw it again.

A word, finally, on pigeon shooting. Whilst the pigeon has been granted an open season it is not, as far as I am concerned, a game bird and shooting it is a close season activity. This being said, I fully realise it is an important quarry species for very many and in no way am I attempting to demean their sport.

For me the best pigeon shooting is roost shooting in early spring. A cold, blustery evening in February or March is ideal. Under a leaden sky the flight starts early and can continue until it is almost completely dark. In the swirling wind one can be presented with some magnificent snap shots between the tree tops. An added bonus on a windy evening is that the shots die and so do not alert approaching birds. My preference is for oak woods, preferably isolated so that there are no alternative roosting quarters in the vicinity. Unfortunately oak woodland has become all too scarce in Ireland. That sad state of affairs has now been addressed by recent plantings but it will be a generation or two before the pigeon will come to roost. The beauty of oak woodland for roost flighting is that one can stand at the edge of a small clearing in the vicinity of a few large and inviting ivy-clad trees. The next best thing to an oak wood, in my estimation, is a mature larch plantation. The trees are tall, so guaranteeing high birds and, though they are close together, visibility is quite good. Again, one can do one's shooting in the wood.

In the case of conifer plantations one is usually confined to flighting incoming birds at the edge. There are evenings when one can be lucky and pick up a good flight line. More often than not though they tend to come in on a broad front. The only answer then is a line of guns sited at strategic intervals.

Decoying pigeons over drilled corn or stubbles is one of the very few forms of wing shooting to which I have never been able to warm. It can be fast and furious at times but too many of the birds fail to deliver a challenging shot. I find that, as the number of 'decoys' increases with the slain, pigeons tend to become increasingly suicidal. On occasions, apparently oblivious to the banging, they will follow in a falling bird as if it were one pitching in to feed. I suspect that if I were more skilful in the art of locating hides I could engineer better shooting, good crossing birds for example instead of a stream coming in from the front with their wings open.

I think that my problem with the pigeon, if the truth be known, is that I have been spoiled since childhood by living in an area with a great variety of game. When one can walk out of one's own back door and start shooting snipe and golden plover within one hundred yards, or drive a few short miles in search of woodcock, duck and grouse, it is hard to put the pigeon very high on the priority list. I am undoubtedly being grossly unfair to the poor bird.

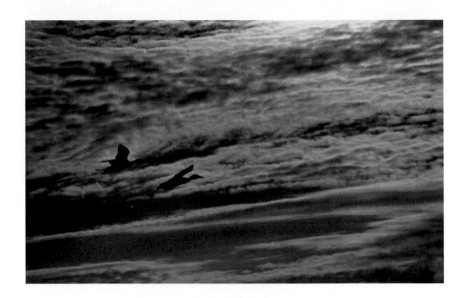

September at Last

For lovers of genuinely wild game, 1st September is a glorious day on the Irish shooting calendar. Seasons open for grouse, eleven species of duck, snipe, jack snipe and golden plover. These all extend to 31st January except in the case of grouse for which shooting is confined to the month of September.

Grouse shooting used to start on 12th August. Then, during the 1970s, a chaotic situation was orchestrated by officialdom. The opening date was put back to 1st September for the western counties and left on 12th August for those in the east. This, allegedly, was because the cool, moist springs typical of the western seaboard were resulting in a later hatch and too many immature grouse in August. For a country as small as Ireland this made precious little sense. Eventually, in 1979, 1st September was appointed as the opening day throughout the Republic. However, another anomaly remained. In Northern Ireland 12th August was retained as the opening date – and very sensibly too. August is the month to shoot grouse and they are virtually always ready by the 12th. We now have the crazy situation in which it is legitimate to shoot grouse on one part of a moor but not on another. This happens, for example, on the heather-covered uplands where counties Monaghan and Tyrone meet.

Grouse, it should be pointed out, refers solely to red grouse. As far as I am aware there is no evidence to suggest that black grouse ever resided in Ireland. When the last Ice Age ended some ten thousand years ago the red grouse was one of the first birds to colonize the country. It may well be that the black grouse would have come as well if the rising waters had not restored the country's island status. England was still attached to the European mainland at that time and thus the final destination for quite a lot of species returning from the warmer south. Ireland's last land bridge which had joined it to southern Scotland was by now well submerged. For this reason quite a number of creatures that are a familiar sight in the English countryside are absent from Ireland. Green woodpeckers, nuthatches, moles and grass snakes are examples.

The red grouse was formerly thought to be a species confined to Ireland and Britain. And Irish birds, on account of their lighter plumage, were treated as a separate sub-species. It is now recognised however that the red grouse is but one of a number of races of the Scandinavian willow grouse. In plumage Irish grouse are most similar to those of the Hebrides. My grouse shooting outside Ireland has been confined to these western isles of Scotland and certainly the birds that I shoot there are very similar to our own.

But similar as they are in appearance I have always been very conscious on my visits to the Hebrides of one rather different behavioural characteristic. It is a very rare occasion upon which an Irish grouse will allow itself to be seen on the ground. Looking back over the years I can only think of two or three such occasions. One is etched firmly and forever in my mind. There is a smallish hill at the back of our mountains, some 1,300 feet in height, which has a flat plateau at the top and which is usually good for a covey or two of grouse. I think it suits them because it always seems to have a good heather mix, a couple of bog holes which never go dry and an abundance of grit. Geography dictates that I usually approach this hill from the east, its steepest side. Unlike the top, the flanks of the hill are covered with tall, ancient heather. The combination of gradient and rough growth means a tough climb from the valley beneath. Having made the ascent I usually stop to draw breath about twenty feet below the plateau. The dogs, who are usually at least twice as fit, know that they must not poke their snouts over the top until I can breathe normally again.

On the afternoon in question I had taken the short usual rest and was in the process of completing the climb. As my head and shoulders came over the skyline I was conscious of something different about the plateau. My first thought was that someone had erected a fence as I could see what appeared to be a row of stake. Then I realised what the 'stakes' were. A covey of eight or nine grouse had been feeding in a line. When this human apparition appeared I think that they must have stretched up their necks to see what was happening. In that milli-second of my recognition the 'stakes' rose as one and flew away.

Pointing and setting dogs make it very clear that grouse are close. Despite this I have

The edge of the mountain where, in former times, the habitat of grey partridge and red grouse overlapped.

never seen an Irish grouse in the heather in front of a dog. In contrast, there was many a time in the Hebrides when the dog was on point and a line of heads could be seen weaving away through the heather. I always felt that those Hebridean birds were just that little bit less inclined to take to the air than our birds here.

Even on the better Irish grouse mountains, grouse densities are relatively low. This means that a very good dog is essential. If one is going to walk many miles in a day, and I mean many miles, fifteen or twenty would not be exceptional, it is imperative that the few chances that come one's way have a satisfactory conclusion.

I think that it is more a question of accident than design that one favours a pointer as opposed to a setter. I actually started shooting grouse, when I was young and very fit, using springers. I would not recommend this to anyone. It requires the degree of fitness of an Olympic gold medal winner to shoot grouse successfully whilst running across rough terrain. I had, though, one springer which brought me a lot of success with grouse.

Her name was Kim and she came to me as a five-year-old. What made her a great grouse dog was the fact that she suffered from a delusion that she was really a setter. It may well have been that some setter genes had found their way into her forebears. A normal springer, when contact with game is imminent, indicates this fact with an exuberant burst into the cover, excitement visible in every sinew of its being. Kim was different. The excitement engendered in her by a grouse's proximity would cause her to go down on her belly and drag herself silently to the point of contact. This nearly always gave me time to get up before she remembered that she was, after all, a springer and hurled herself into the clump of heather. In old age her delusions became more pronounced and I

39

can recall at least one occasion when I had to knee her into the flush. My greatest regret was that I never got a litter from her. I only tried once and that was probably too late. At the appropriate time I took Kim to meet a gentleman springer of distinction and left her for a few days. On her return home she was duly locked up for a while. Eventually the whinging became too much; she was not used to incarceration, and in a moment of weakness I let her out. That was a major mistake. Looking out the window less than an hour later I saw a local mongrel paying his respects. In a fit of rage I broke a broom handle across his back. This succeeded in cooling his ardour but the deed was done. A few weeks later Kim was delivered of a most unspringer-like litter of pups.

Kim passed away suddenly one early August morning. In those years grouse shooting started on 12th August so I had a serious problem. Pure chance intervened and I became a lifelong pointer man. I heard of a man who had a two-year-old pointer for sale. By coincidence he lived very near my favourite grouse territory. The dog's name was Bruce and, after the most inauspicious of beginnings, he developed into the best pointer that I have ever owned. When I made contact with his owner he suggested that I take the dog on the hill for a trial. Most of our grouse shooting involves an initial climb through a plantation. On the day of Bruce's trial I had hardly left the trees when, twenty yards ahead, he froze on top of a turf bank, clearly indicating that there was something exciting below. I was highly impressed. At least until, on my command, he leaped over the bank and took off across the heather in hot pursuit of a mountain sheep. For some unaccountable reason I decided to keep going. Bruce was a revelation. He did everything right. He quartered

Mallard in a wildfowl sanctuary in winter. Note that their heads are up. All humanity is now treated with grave suspicion.

ahead of me, pointed grouse and remained on point until I kneed him in the behind. A deal was soon done. Fifty pounds changed hands, a princely sum in those days, and Bruce was mine. He lived to the age of twelve and gave me enormous pleasure year after year.

One incident in his first year with us could have ruined a beautiful relationship if Bruce had been a lesser dog. It was early November and my youngest son, six at the time, was out with me on his very first day's shooting. We were searching for pheasants and Bruce soon came on point at the edge of an exceptionally thick patch of blackthorns. In order to get round to the point at which the pheasant would emerge I had to make a bit of a detour. I instructed the son to wait until I whistled and then give the bushes a kick. Bruce could be a little sticky on occasions and this was always a sure way of getting him into a cover. I suppose the bird moved slightly at the noise and so set him going. I took up my position and whistled. Almost immediately there was pandemonium. A dull thud was followed by a high pitched yelping as the cock pheasant and Bruce came out at knots. Clearly wires had got crossed. It transpired that my son had thought that the instruction was to kick the dog when I whistled. So there was Bruce, doing his job as diligently as ever, when out of the blue he was the recipient of a mighty root up the backside from a sturdy six-year-old.

Other Pointers and Two Difficult Setters

After Bruce I had a number of pointers, all good journeymen but nowhere near his class. Only twice did I own a setter. On the first occasion, as had been the case with the death of Kim, I lost a dog shortly before the season. Unable to lay hands on a suitable pointer, I bought a very handsome lemon and white setter that promised much when I took her on trial. She was a fine dog but a lot stickier than the pointers to which I had grown accustomed. Once she had found grouse I would have to walk round her and flush them myself. In fairness she was as good as any pointer when it came to finding birds. My other setter was a large and rather clumsy dog called Rusty. He was an Irish Setter given to me by a cousin. Rusty had severe psychological problems and only half understood what his role in life was really about. He could find grouse and pheasants, of that there was no doubt. The trouble was that on reaching the bird's final hiding place he would start to bark furiously rather than do the more conventional setter thing.

In 1999 I was given a small and lively two-year-old pointer. Glen quickly proved to be something special. Despite his slightly frail appearance he quartered the mountain with style and was as steady as a rock whenever he found birds. As his first season with me passed my regard for him increased: he was nearly in Bruce's class. He served me well up until the end of the 2004/5 season. Shortly after the end of the season his weight started to fall away and in no time at all he died of bone cancer. Those who have spent long hours in the field with a dog, be it springer, setter or pointer, will know only too well the sense of loss that accompanies its passing. A new relationship is not built overnight.

For those of us fortunate enough to live in a part of the country in which it is possible to hunt both grouse and duck, 1st September brings with it a delicious dilemma. Should the first shots of the new season be discharged across the purple heather or at black silhouettes circling bog or stubbles in the first light of dawn?

There is no more avid hunter of duck than me. The whistling of wigeon or the piping of teal at evening flight still thrill me as they did long ago when, single-barrelled gun in hand, I first waited by a grassy splash. But, when it comes to a question of grouse or duck there is no contest. The grouse is the aristocrat of the game bird world, its pursuit in the high wildernesses is for me the pinnacle of our sport. For many years 1st September would find me climbing towards the heather well before daybreak. I always aimed to be in grouse territory by the time that it was bright enough to shoot a rising bird. My long-suffering wife would drive me to my usual starting point at the very back of the mountains. From there, well equipped with sandwiches to last the day, I would set off on a hike that would bring me right across the hills. At the far side the same good lady would be waiting around 5pm to ferry me home. After a large meal the final act of opening day was evening flight. Sometimes, with the excitement of the day, I would be in the heather too early. On one occasion I can recall walking into a small covey so early that they had disappeared into the glooming before I had time to shoulder the gun. Those were always special days and, considering the time of year, the weather was nearly always fine. When my sons reached their early teens they would accompany me. The only difference was that now there were a number of crumpled bodies to be collected at day's end instead of the usual one. We always followed approximately the same route. When you really get to know a mountain range it becomes second nature to visit some parts and avoid others. This being said there will always be times when grouse spring from the most unexpected of places. Most likely they have been driven there by some predator or another party of hunters.

On those long safaris there would be periods when the dog could find absolutely nothing. Occasionally a slight change in demeanour would bring short-lived hope, usually dashed when a meadow pipit fluttered from the heather. Our mountains seem to hold enormous numbers of these little birds. I suspect that they are the main food of the merlins and hen harriers that patrol the moors. It is my experience that the best of dogs, after a long and grouseless walk, will begin to take an increasing interest in pipits. Maybe they are just relieving their boredom. A good friend, who shall remain nameless for fear that he night otherwise become an ex-friend if identified, possesses a setter of which he is inordinately proud. It has unusual and individualistic ideas about quartering. Not for it the humdrum routine of traversing back and forth across the heather some hundred yards ahead. At times it simply disappears and, after much eye straining, one sees a motionless white object on a distant hill. Half walking, half running we reach the site of potential action. The hound moves forward. A covey of grouse may tear from the heather. Equally, a meadow pipit may make a disdainful appearance. The problem is that one cannot take a chance. After a couple of pipits the next sett might well produce a rather larger, redder bird.

There is nothing like strenuous mountain work to generate a real appetite. Especially if there are few birds in the area there is no more simple pleasure than lying back in luxuriant heather and getting stuck into the sandwiches. More than once this simple pleasure has resulted in the unexpected. The relaxation in the heather is inevitably accompanied by a certain amount of noise and general banter. Under such circumstance, one might think, no self-respecting grouse would stay anywhere near. Yet there have been times when someone has asked the question, 'Where's the dog?' And there he is, no more than fifty yards away on as firm a point as one could wish to see. A sudden silence descends. Sandwiches and thermos flasks go to the four winds. Guns and cartridges are clawed for. Will the grouse have the basic decency to stay a while longer? Once, in one of those golden moments, everything went right. We walked quietly across to where Bruce stood motionless and shot four out of four. Seldom do the Gods allow such things to happen.

I had a similar and most extraordinary experience one balmy August evening. In those days, grouse shooting opened on 12th August. I had escaped the many demands of everyday life and had a few hours to spend on the hill. My objective that evening was a lovely flat

A brace of grouse about to be plucked.

moor which borders on a little-used road. When time is of the essence it is an ideal place because one can park the car on a disused turf road and get straight into the heather. In those days there were far fewer people shooting so there was always a good chance of a bird or two. Nowadays it is over shot because it is just too accessible and I no longer bother to visit it. On the evening in question there was a car parked on the turf road when I arrived. At first I assumed that I had been beaten to the draw and thought about seeking an alternative venue. However, inspection of the car did not suggest that it had transported any doggy passengers. So I set off across the moor with the ever-faithful Bruce strutting his stuff. I then had a double surprise.

There in the heather were two nuns enjoying a picnic in the warm evening sunshine. Next to them Bruce was very firmly indicating that I should come over and shoot some grouse. He was no more than twenty five or thirty yards from the nuns. This was a situation to which a mere mortal like myself should not have been subjected. The nuns were already eyeing me with more than a passing suspicion. Could I in all honesty discharge a couple of barrels in such close proximity? As matters transpired the answer was yes. Before I had any time for decision-making, a covey of eleven birds rose from the heather. Because of the extraordinary circumstances, I suppose, I hesitated. This is invariably fatal with wing shooting because the automatic eye-hand coordination is momentarily lost. But then the blood lust of the hunter took over and I fired a single shot. Nothing fell. The covey were clearly not unduly disturbed and, after gliding a few hundred yards, they landed on the side of a very small hill upon which, long ago, turf cutting took place. Without daring to glance over my shoulder to see what the nuns were doing I took off in hot pursuit. The evening had a happy ending for me. Bruce quickly found the

43

covey, and despite their number they had landed quite close together, so I was presented with an easy right and left. Further on I added another grouse to the bag. On my return, a couple of hours later the nuns had gone. Unsurprisingly, I never met then there again.

Small things can make or mar a day on the hills. A simple act of omission once provided me with an opening day which I will never forget. My two eldest sons, who were about twelve and fourteen at the time, were there with me. We had just been dropped off at our usual starting point around 6am. As the car disappeared into the distance it suddenly dawned on me that the normal lavish quantities of food and drink were missing from my bag.

No panic though, they were surely stowed in one of the boys' bags. A hopeful enquiry elicited the sad information. We had not so much as a bar of chocolate between the three of us. Ten or eleven hours of tough walking and climbing lay ahead. Never did a day pass more slowly. To make matters worse the grouse were in a singularly unobliging mood. The only sustenance available were bilberries, or whorts as we call them. These are small, dark blue berries borne on scrubby plants that grow in profusion on parts of the mountains. Whorts are sweet and succulent but suffer from one serious deficiency. They contain a purple juice which stains everything with which it comes in contact. In the absence of any other food the temptation to stop and pick a few whorts grows stronger the longer one is on the hill. The result is predictable: purple hands, purple lips and purple tongue. On that fateful day three well-stained individuals finally crept gratefully into the car.

On those occasions when the grouse fail to oblige, the odd hint or two of their presence can be sufficient to make the day. It may be a neat little heap of greyish green droppings or a few mottled feathers in the heather. The important thing is that there are grouse about. There

Fresh feathers on a flight pond at dawn – always a welcome sight.

will be another day. A family of grouse will tend to spend their time in a relatively small area, maybe only a few acres, if they are not unduly disturbed or forced to leave because of drought or some other untoward meteorological event.

Nowadays I no longer head for the hill at dawn on 1st September. There will be plenty of time for early morning forays later in the month. For no particular reason that I can recall, a few of us decided to leave the first assault on the grouse until later in the morning. As a result we all go our own ways at dawn in search of duck. We then meet up at around 10am. At this hour yet another long-suffering wife dishes up a quite enormous breakfast that goes a long way towards sustaining us for the remainder of the day. There is then the annual photograph of the group. Depending upon the year, between six and nine set out on this first pilgrimage of the new season. Our route is more or less the same each opening day.

In theory the ensuing campaign should run smoothly. The guns line up along a fire break at the edge of the heather some forty yards apart. Between them the dogs await their orders to begin quartering. Rarely however does theory translate into practice on the mountain. Fitness, or rather lack of it, is a perennial problem. Twenty minutes into the heather the signs of a summer of inactivity become all too apparent. The straight line is, to put it mildly, more than a little on the crooked side. This crookedness becomes exacerbated by the nature of the terrain. At any one moment the line might be ascending a steep gradient, going round the side of a hill or straddling a mixture of flat and hilly ground. Following the side of a hill is the most difficult when it comes to trying to keep the line straight. The man at the top has the shortest journey whilst his colleague a few hundred yards lower is under continuous pressure to

Plenty of barley in the shallows, irresistible to mallard and teal. Wigeon can also develop a love of grain.

keep in line. Should the heather be on the damp slippery side it is a full time job just keeping one's balance especially if the gradient is steep.

Then there are the dogs. Inevitably a motley collection of pointers, setters, labradors and at least one of slightly uncertain pedigree. One thing is certain. No grouse will be left skulking in the heather. Less certain is whether, on finding birds, the same motley collection will have the collective good grace to remain frozen until the guns arrive. In my experience if one dog makes a find the next to arrive will also come on point. Matters become rather less than predictable when the rest of the pack arrives. It only takes the tiniest modicum of jealousy to precipitate a mini disaster. There have been times when threats of summary execution have been issued. The moral of the story is, should one see a dog on point, get there quickly and the devil take the hindmost.

On our mountains everyone is confronted with a tough climb at fairly regular intervals. Such is the nature of upland shooting. In my case some variation of Murphy's Law seems to come into operation when I am confronted with a gradient of one in five or steeper. Less than half way to the top and lungs bursting, I look up to see a dog pointing a few hundred feet above me. A fitter colleague, there is always at least one, is already on hand and is making furious gestures for me to get there fast.

The colleague is not going to wait too long. Hence I must make the ascent at knots and, gasping for breath, take my chances when the dogs move in. A grouse shot under these circumstances is a grouse well and truly earned.

We do not usually shoot that many grouse on this first expedition. A combination of deplorable fitness levels, slightly wayward dogs and more chatter than there should be on the shooting field combine to give the birds a better than evens chance. Indeed it could be said with some degree of truth that this first outing is a fine demonstration of the noble art of conservation.

When the day is done another meal awaits, provided by the same good lady who plied us with sausages, black puddings and all other manner of goodies earlier in the day. A few balls of malt may be consumed whilst awaiting and during the feast. And after it as well. Then it is decision time. Those not totally shattered by early rising and a day of unaccustomed energy expenditure must opt for pond or stubbles. Lesser mortals are already asleep upon the sofa.

After the opening day we get together as a group once or twice more. It is difficult enough to find a day that suits everyone on account of work and other commitments. We are effectively confined to weekends, as is the case with heather burning. And again like heather burning the weather has a major bearing on proceedings. Those of us lucky enough to have more time on our hands may make a solo run or two. If the weather forecast is promising a small group of two or three may make arrangements at short notice. Some years the weather in September is less than benign so it is important to make the most of any decent spells that come along.

Weather conditions probably impact on grouse shooting in mountainous regions more than on any other form of game shooting. Even during dry spells low cloud and mist can persist until quite late on a September morning. Walking up a forest path with a steady drip from the spruce needles wetting the hair, one is inclined to make a silent prayer that the forecasters are right and that within the hour the heather will be bathed in sunlight. Those initial climbs through the forestry are rarely without incident. It may be a pair of ravens complaining loudly at this unwarranted intrusion into their domain. Or it might be a surprised young fallow buck crashing away through the bracken. Sometimes the dog will find a pheasant. It never ceases to amaze me how high up a mountain pheasants can and do live. Not infrequently I come across a hen with a late brood at well over a thousand feet. There is one rock-strewn hill where the heather only grows well in patches. Despite its unpromising appearance it normally holds a few grouse. Towards the end of September last year we counted 26 one wet afternoon. For some reason this hill always carries a few pheasants as well. If we do not meet them at the forest's edge there is every chance that the dogs will flush them out of the heather.

Many years ago I took to this hill a friend who had expressed an interest in shooting a grouse. We managed to get separated and for a while lost sight of one another. This is a not an uncommon experience on those breezy days when banks of cloud swirl in suddenly from the south west and, just as suddenly, are gone again. The cloud was just lifting when I heard a single shot. Minutes later my friend was walking over to me, face wreathed in smiles. 'So you got one', I commented. 'Yes', said he, 'A fine cock.' He then proceeded to pull a large cock pheasant from his bag. So delighted was he with his trophy that I had not the heart to tell him that the pheasant season was not due to open for another six weeks.

On those mornings on which the mist is slow to clear one can tramp the heather for hours without coming across the slightest indication of grouse. Scenting conditions are poor and even the best dogs can become dispirited. Just occasionally though one can get lucky. One opening morning we had been walking like lost souls in fairly dense low cloud. It was showing little sign of lifting and we were giving serious thought to abandoning the proceedings when a covey of five or six grouse appeared out of nowhere and alighted in the heather not much more than a hundred

47

yards away. It was only a matter of walking over quietly and opening our account for the day. I once had a similar experience at high altitude. High altitude means over two thousand feet in this part of the world. Two of us had decided upon an early morning climb to a spot which regularly holds a covey. The mist was just beginning to lighten when some sixth sense caused us to look up. Sailing high over my partner's head was a pair of grouse. He reacted too late, not that I would have done any better, and fired two ineffectual shots. What happened next could not have been predicted. The grouse, which had crossed some hundred feet above us, in an outrageous display of contempt for our shooting skills, proceeded to land just down the hill. They paid the ultimate price for that show of contempt.

Good duck habitat in County Tipperary.

There have been other occasions when I have seen grouse flying in low cloud. The most unlucky grouse that I ever met was one that was totally disorientated. It had been a day when the forecasters got it badly wrong. Instead of the promised sunshine the morning grew steadily more and more misty. I decided that the only sane course was to get back to the car as quickly as possible. There were two ways of doing so. Option one was a long hike through light rain and drizzle around the side of the mountain. Option two was straight over the top where the rain was getting heavier. I decided upon option two. Squelching along, soaked to the skin, I encountered two birds. The first was a raven which was clearly lost. It followed me for a while. I have often wondered whether it saw me as a means of deliverance or as a potential meal. I thought about shooting it. Maybe some form of telepathy then came into play because when I looked up again the raven was gone. Not long afterwards I heard what can only be described as a squawk. Not twenty yards away, battling into the now-driving rain, was a grouse. To my eternal shame I shot it. After all, that was my purpose in this lonesome place! It was a magnificent old cock in full plumage with the longest white socks that I had ever seen.

During periods of really settled weather a mountain day is likely to have one of two beginnings. Either the sunlight streams across the entire mountain as dawn breaks or mist persists lower down until it is burned off by the heat of the day. In the latter case an early climb to the high ground is not dissimilar to taking off in an aeroplane on a foggy day. The plantation is dank and cool and visibility is poor. Little changes during the early part of the ascent. Then, usually not too far out into the heather, there is a brightness in the mist. Minutes later one is standing in brilliant sunshine, with all below swathed in white. Ahead lie countless acres of purple heather shimmering in the early morning light. There is the inevitable breeze of altitude and scenting conditions are good. The dogs are impatient to go about their business. Assuredly such days were specially designed with grouse shooting in mind.

The grouse shooters of another generation would never have dreamed of being on the hill at such an unearthly hour. This was not on account of a surfeit of postprandial port though, mind you, over-indulgence on the night proceeding a tough day on the hill is not to

be recommended. I cannot personally vouch for this if the tipple is port but I have some experience in the case of whiskey. A throbbing head and a dry mouth definitely do not add to the pleasures of high ground sport. In fact they do not add to the pleasures of low ground sport either.

Those hunters of former eras took the view that the time to shoot grouse was on a sunny afternoon. There was some logic in their thinking. Grouse, they would argue, feed from dawn onwards. At this time of day they are perilously exposed on short, young heather and, like all feeding birds, are restless and have one eye on the sky for predators. Living in a covey means that the pecking order principle applies and so there is always an extra degree of awareness of approaching threats. In a nutshell it is no easy matter to approach feeding grouse. Far better, these gentlemen believed, to wait until the birds had eaten their fill and retired to the security of high heather to rest and digest the contents of their crops. Hard to argue with this. But these same gentlemen lived at a time when grouse were abundant and only the privileged shot. They could easily fill their bags in the course of an afternoon.

It is certainly a fact that grouse move to cover as an early autumn day runs its course. It is also a fact that they can be more easily approached towards evening. I can remember many a day when, totally despondent, we had been walking back to the car after a long and grouseless hike. Then, out of the blue, one of the despondent brethren notices that the dogs have made a find. Drooping spirits are quickly revived and the day is saved at the eleventh hour.

One of my fondest memories is of such a day in late September. There were seven of us in the party, two of whom had never seen a grouse, let alone shot one. It had been very hot and our long safari began and ended at a broken forestry gate which was supposed to stop sheep from entering the plantation.

Less than fifty yards from the gate there is a triangle of land, not much more than one third of an acre in extent, bounded by three fire breaks. I do no think that anyone has ever bothered to burn the heather in this triangle. We never bother to walk through it as it is something of a mini jungle. It must have been around 6pm when we arrived back. We were

hot, tired and a little on the growly side. All thoughts of meeting a grouse had long since left our minds.

Coming up to the triangle the three dogs that accompanied us that day, and which by now were as dispirited as ourselves, suddenly came to life. In no time at all the three of them were rigid. My immediate thought was that a single old cock bird would shortly make an appearance. We tend to meet these old bachelors right at the edge of the heather. But this was no singleton. The dogs moved in and flushed a fine covey. There were at least ten birds and probably more. I shot one but failed to register a second. At each attempt to fire another barrel I was beaten to the draw and my intended target was already on the way down. Best of all our two novices got a bird each. We picked five birds but could not find a sixth that had been shot by one of the novices. As diligently as we searched we could not find it. Under other circumstance we would have given up but this was a man's first grouse. One last sweep and there it was. How we had missed it I will never know. The grouse was lying on its back on a newly bulldozed fire break, as obvious as could be. I can still see that man's face. Despair had turned to elation. He was holding the grouse lovingly in two hands and it was clearly a very special moment.

If one is not already a creature of habit, a life devoted to rough shooting will certainly remedy that deficiency. In any given area it does

'Willow' doing her thing. She is a very small but unbelievably courageous water-dog.

50

not take long to learn where the likely spots are and the places which are not worth a visit. As a result a day's itinerary is to some extent preordained. This is especially true of our grouse shooting because of the brevity of the season and the vagaries of the weather. The object of the exercise is to bag a few bird so, with limited opportunities, why forsake the tried and trusted? Sounds sensible but such thinking ignores one essential. By pandering to one's more conservative instincts and always shooting the same general areas, one is more likely to condition the intended quarry to fade away more quickly when their patch is invaded. This is one reason, I suspect, why prime territory can fail to deliver the goods on occasions.

I have to confess that my travels across the hills are quite predictable. According to the amount of time available, and the likelihood of heavy showers, full day, half day and shorter campaign routes have evolved over the years. They have one thing in common. Along each of them are patches of heather which will disappoint if they do not at the very least elicit some expression of interest from the dogs. More often than not I would expect at least one of these special places to come good. The downside is that such places are generally separated by much lower quality ground. The secret is to keep one's concentration because even in the most unlikely of spots a grouse can appear when the mind is far away.

GROUSE IN HIGH PLACES

Down the years I have discovered two very special places. One of these, alas, has ceased to be even slightly special. It is a flat area between two hills which lies not much more than one thousand feet above sea level. Covering some five hundred acres, it has near its centre a very rough area with a number of turf banks moulded over centuries by driving wind and rain. For years the immediate area of the turf banks proved irresistible to grouse. Season after season there would be two coveys in residence when the shooting season opened. Quite abruptly everything changed. Nowadays the best that can be expected there is the odd bird or two. It may have been totally coincidental but the change took place around the time that an international boy scout jamboree spent a few nights under canvas in that part of the mountains. No disrespect intended to a noble organisation but the sheer level of disturbance may have persuaded the residents to move elsewhere.

The second venue rarely disappoints. I think that I can honestly say that is has provided me with more great moments than any other of the countless places in which I have hunted grouse. It is located at the bottom of a hill where the gradient gradually eases. Across it runs an ancient stony track. Why this track was laid I have no idea. It is literally in the middle of nowhere and does not appear to serve any obvious purpose. The grouse use this track for gritting and a liberal amount of droppings usually betrays their presence. Year in year out the heather here has a richness which distinguishes it from the heather of the surrounding areas. Here and there irregular heaps of old red sandstone protrude through the heather.

The best way to reach this place without disturbing the grouse is to make a long detour around the stony and unproductive flank of the mountain. By so doing one arrives at a point at just the right level. Dropping down to good grouse ground from a height is never to be recommended. Equally, having to climb puts one at a disadvantage as it is not easy to swing sweetly when the breathing is laboured.

I will share but three memories of this most sacred of spots. It was not my intention, in penning these lines, to embarrass any of my friends by mentioning them by name. However, I am going to make one exception. The man's name is Stanley and he is, without question, the finest sportsman that it has ever been my pleasure to know. When he was in his late fifties

Stanley had two hip replacement operations. Notwithstanding this he continued to walk the mountains. Indeed he covered distances and terrain which would deter all but the more dedicated younger men. On the day of which I write we had, as so often in the past, walked hard and long for little return. We had started at dawn and had been rewarded by no more than a brace of grouse. Near to 4pm we came to the aforementioned sacred spot. Because of the undulating nature of the place we lost sight of one another. Two quick shots then told me that Stanley had struck lucky. At the second shot I felt a stinging pain in the small of my back caused, presumably, by a stray grain. Stanley is the most meticulous and careful of shooters. Swinging round I was surprised to see a grouse heading straight for me. It had however seen me and rapidly changed course. The resulting going away shot was not a particularly difficult one. Collecting the grouse I walked over to where I had heard the shots. Stanley had two birds down and was searching for the second one. His pointer, Floyd, had gone AWOL. After a long search we found the second bird. The next job was to find Floyd who had still not returned.

He was much nearer than we realised, standing resolutely on point in some very high heather. Two grouse got up and we shot one each. Shortly afterwards Stanley put the cap on a great day by adding a further bird to the bag.

The Path of the Shotgun Pellet

I learned an important lesson that day. Despite a lifetime of shooting I had never realised just how far a shotgun pellet can travel and still retain its damaging striking force. Having retrieved the bird that I had shot, I paced the distance to the point from which the pellet which hit me had been fired. It was approximately two hundred yards. So much for my long-held belief that a shotgun will kill at up to fifty or sixty yards and maybe carry for about twice that distance.

A few years later a friend and I came to this place by the same route. It had been a long hot day and we were tired and disgruntled and had not fired a single shot. Just at that point where stony ground and heather meet, Bruce came to an abrupt halt. A strong covey of about eight or nine took wing and we shot three. My friend, delighted at getting a right and left, picked up his birds and gleefully threw himself into the heather for a well-earned rest. For some strange reason, for I was as tired as he, I kept walking. Bruce had moved on from the scene of the previous action and was, almost immediately, showing serious intent once again. He pointed less than one hundred yards from where the previous covey had risen. This time a smaller covey, six I think, got up and I shot two. My friend, still lying in the heather, could only watch. I enjoyed the moment. It is nice, if a little unchristian, to wipe a colleague's eye. Such is the nature of rough shooting. Hours of unrewarded walking are soon forgotten when good fortune briefly intervenes.

Three years ago I was out on my own on a day of rapidly changing weather. Bright sunshine and squally showers were appearing and disappearing with equal rapidity. It was very reminiscent of the Hebrides and their unique brand of Atlantic weather. There were nights on those lovely islands when we would be awakened in the early hours by the noise of rain hopping off the slates. It seemed inconceivable that we would be shooting the following day. Yet, come dawn, the sun would be shining and the deluge of the night no more than a distant memory.

That morning, once again, I had walked hard and long without meeting a grouse. My companion was Glen. The complexion of this part of the mountain had changed quite drastically since my previous visit because of some serious heather burning. There were some

Willow waits patiently for a wounded duck to re-surface. At times like this a good gundog is an essential companion.

nice expanses of regrowth but not a great deal of old heather. The available cover consisted of a few patches of the old heather and one long strip about five yards in depth. I think that these odd pieces survive because, as the heather burns along a broad front, a sudden gust of wind temporarily changes the direction of the flames.

The remaining strip of heather was next to a broad expanse of young growth. As we crossed the young heather it was clear that Glen knew that we were not alone. At the junction of young and old growth two things happened simultaneously. Glen stopped and pointed and an old cock grouse burst into the air. Before the sound of my shot had died a big covey, at least ten birds, was airborne. Readers unfamiliar with grouse will notice that I am often imprecise as to the exact size of a covey. There is a simple reason for this. When a covey rises events seem to occur with quite extraordinary rapidity. First one lines up a particular bid and then, if successful, moves on to a second. The rest of the covey are, at best, a fleeting impression.

I shot a second bird which fell some distance away. This was the one situation with which Glen never really learned to cope. Two birds in the heather, one near and one far. Having picked up the first he would set off in search of the second, in the process dropping the first. I would therefore have to keep a sharp eye on him as, once a bird is dropped, it is no easy task to find it in a sea of heather. I was in the process of running down to where I thought the bird had been dropped when a whirr of wings caused me to stop and turn. A single grouse was rising high, more after the manner of a pheasant than a grouse. This is not an uncommon happening when a covey is disturbed. One of its number stays behind. Why this should happen I have no idea. Experience teaches one to re-load immediately in order to take advantage of this situation. This becomes almost a reflex action and on this particular day I literally did not know whether or not I had reloaded. I pulled on the grouse and it fell to earth. That was my only contact with grouse that day but it was more than sufficient.

Psychologists tell us that we store the pleasant memories of childhood and jettison most of the less pleasant ones. Weather and school holidays are a classic example. We remember well the long hot summers, which were generally scarce commodities, but have little memory of the wet and miserable ones. Much the same, I think, holds true for shooting memories. The great days, when everything went right, can be recalled in minute detail. But who wants to remember those all-too-frequent ones, especially on the mountain, when the heavens opened and bedraggled humanity was washed back to the valley. To be honest getting wet, indeed very wet, is a fairly regular part of the grouse shooting scene. Many a day we have set off more in hope than anything else that the forecasters had got it wrong. More often than not we should have had greater faith in these good people.

Many sights and sounds add to the pleasure of a day on the mountains. Ravens are rarely far away, tumbling in the sky or uttering their raucous calls. Once in a while a merlin darts from the heather or a hen harrier flaps lazily across the moor. Very occasionally I have disturbed a peregrine falcon feeding on the ground. Each time its prey was a racing pigeon. Swallows engage in non-stop flight above September heather. It always amazes me that there should be such a wealth of insect life available for them at this altitude.

THE CALL OF THE GOLDEN PLOVER

One of the evocative sounds of the mountain is the call of the golden plover. It has rightly been described as plaintive. No sound more epitomizes the wildness of the surroundings than that liquid, gurgling whistle. As a breeding species the golden plover has declined very considerably in Ireland. Many of its former moorland breeding grounds have been lost as a result of afforestation. The resident population is now no more than a few hundred pairs.

These nest at scattered locations in a few western and north-western counties. In winter however hundreds of thousands of golden plovers descend upon the country. Most of them come from Iceland.

In my estimation the golden plover is one of the most underestimated of game birds. It is elusive, fast of wing and performs with distinction on the dining table. All things, in fact, that a game bird should be. The first migrants arrive as early as mid-August but it is usually September before we meet many of them. They add interest and variety on a shooting day. When golden plover first arrive they tend to make for the stony ground above the heather line. Another favoured haunt is recently burned ground on which regrowth has not yet started. In such places one will sometimes see them around running in that unique, erratic manner of their kind as they search and probe for insects. More usually they are heard before they are seen. Then, with a rush of wings a pack swings low across the heather and is lost from sight as quickly as it appeared. The pack may consist of a dozen birds or less, or there may be several hundred. There is always a temptation to brown the pack. Needless to say this practice has little to do with sportsmanship and should be avoided. This being said, if one is fortunate enough to be within range of a pack and pick one's bird, a few are likely to fall simply because they fly so close together.

On an odd occasion we have seen a pack on the ground and tried an impromptu drive. This is far from an easy matter as they are quite likely to swing off in any direction. I cannot recall ever meeting with much success in these cases. One or two birds in the bag would be about par for the course. Days when the cloud is down can provide opportunities to bag a few golden plovers. Under these murky conditions they have a habit of flying around rather aimlessly once disturbed. The whistling betrays them as it gives one the opportunity to be facing in the right direction when a pack emerges from the glooming. Shooting when visibility is poor

BELOW LEFT
Returning home after the rough shoot.

BELOW RIGHT
An easier retrieve than usual.

is always potentially dangerous and is best confined to days when one is alone on the hill or accompanied by a single companion.

By September the plover, though still handsome, have lost the brilliance of their summer plumage. In particular the black breast feathers have been moulted and replaced by a dowdy white. I have only rarely shot a bird that had retained some semblance of its summer finery.

As well as golden plover there are usually a few snipe on the mountain in September. These, I suspect, are the first of the autumn arrivals. Snipe do breed widely in Ireland but I have only found their nests in rushy lowland bogs. As autumn progresses enormous numbers come into the country. Those that we meet in the heather in September rarely give the impression that they are on familiar territory. Their behaviour strongly suggests that they are recent arrivals. When they rise there is just the slightest hint of reluctance about their flight and there is not quite the same wild energy in their departure. Sometimes they will fly no more than a few hundred yards before alighting once more. As September progresses we tend to meet more and more of them. These, I understand, come mainly from Scotland.

On our visit to the Hebrides we always met plenty of snipe. The season in Scotland opens on 12th August and most days we would have half a dozen or more in the bag. I had one upsetting experience there. I can still see the patch of wiry grass where the incident took place. The ever faithful Bruce pointed. I nudged him forward. Nothing happened. More nudging and then, finally, a snipe got up and I shot it. Remarkably, Bruce remained on point. More nudging had no effect so I walked round him and quickly discovered the source of his interest. There in a tussock were four heavily-blotched, pear-shaped eggs. For the only time in my life I had shot a game bird off its nest.

In early autumn the whereabouts of mountain snipe are not always that predictable. Force of habit causes one to detour to wet or rushy patches in the expectation that there will be one or two in residence. Often as not though they have chosen to be elsewhere.

They are just as likely to be flushed from dry heather. Indeed it is not uncommon for a snipe to rise in front of the dog following what one assumed was a grouse find.

JACK AND COMMON SNIPE

We rarely meet jack snipe at this time of year. I think that there are two reasons for this. The first is that they tend to come to Ireland a little later than their larger cousins. As far as I know jack snipe do not breed here. The second is that, unlike the common snipe, they are not so inclined to use the hills as their first point of touchdown. Normally it is easy to distinguish the jack on account of its slower and more direct flight. On the mountain though, mainly because of the wind, the difference is flight between two species is not always that apparent. Often as not the jack has been returned to the heather before one realises that it is a jack.

When the season opens on 1st September grouse shooters set their sights on broadly similar types of terrain. Duck shooters, in contrast, with mallard as their intended quarry, will be spending that first morning in a variety of very different surroundings. Well before dawn one man will be concealing himself in a reed bed at the edge of a lake or slow flowing river. Another will be gathering up the remains of a broken bale of straw in order to construct a hide well out in the stubbles. And yet another, probably accompanied by a long-standing shooting partner, will be waiting until there is sufficient light in the sky to walk the banks of some secluded stream. Most people can find some duck shooting, even if it is only a visit to a favoured local pond.

Some of us are spoiled for choice. My annual dilemma nowadays is whether to flight the barley stubbles — there are some two hundred acres of them behind the house (unfortunately not belonging to me) — or lay in wait in the local bog.

What we call the bog is, in reality, a low lying field from which the water no longer drains away. Over the years the channels through the underlying limestone have become blocked. Reeds and rushes have grown up around the fringes and in the shallower central areas. Essentially it has developed into prime habitat both for breeding and wintering wildfowl. In all, the field extends to twelve or thirteen acres and the greater part of it is submerged. Twenty years ago, before the drainage channels got blocked, the whole place would be as dry as dust in September unless there had been a particularly wet summer. Now all that has changed. It has changed to such a degree that the central marshy islands now provide nesting sites for the biggest colony of black headed gulls in the county.

Less than a mile away is a twenty acre sanctuary lake with a lot of islands. Good numbers of mallard rest on these islands and around the bog. Between the two places, depending upon the year, up to 500 mallard are present in late summer. There is quite a lot of commuting between the two wetlands and the sanctuary quickly fills when the guns open up in September. In spring and early summer the lake provides stark insight into the level of duckling mortality. There is a path all round and one soon gets to know the different broods as they emerge. A few days ago a duck appeared proudly leading her family of nineteen tiny ducklings, one of the biggest hatches I have ever seen. Two days later there were fourteen survivors and a day later the brood was down to ten. If the duck succeeds in retaining half of these she will be doing well. As a general rule the newly hatched broods number between five and ten. Somewhere between twenty and forty percent of these are likely to reach maturity.

I always keep a record of the ratio between young and old mallard

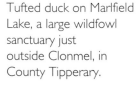

Tufted duck on Marlfield Lake, a large wildfowl sanctuary just outside Clonmel, in County Tipperary.

that I shoot. It is easy to distinguish them by the colour of their paddles. In old birds they are a bright orange whereas in the season's young they are more yellow-orange. I rate it a better than average year if there are three young birds in the bag for every two old ones.

In the 1970s there was a big upsurge in the acreage of winter barley sown in this area. In those days the varieties used had much longer stems than their present day counterparts and lodging was all but inevitable when ripening got underway in early July. The mallard quickly and gratefully discovered these new feeding grounds and small and large parties could be seen moving between the sanctuary lake and the fields all day long. They would become so accustomed to feeding on barley that harvesting activities were not a deterrent. Even when the combines were making their journeys up and down the field the packs would still be circling. Most years they remained faithful to these dining areas right up to September.

Until a few years ago the only other duck in this area in early autumn, with the exception of some very occasional wanderers, were teal. I have never succeeded in finding a nest but there is definitely a small local breeding population. On opening day in the bog there are usually two or three family groups flying around, up to twenty or so birds in all. The experts claim that the Irish breeding population numbers no more than a few hundred pairs. Numbers here gradually build up from late September as the winter visitors begin to come inland.

Twenty five years ago pochard were seldom here before early December. That has changed dramatically of recent times. Figures published in the 1970s suggested that the Irish breeding population consisted of little more than ten pairs. Every few years a single pair would nest on the sanctuary lake and produce a small brood. I never saw the ducklings after the first few days. If they survived they did not stay in the area. Then, about five years ago, we noticed that a few pairs were still in the bog in May. They are now breeding every year which is a great bonus for us. There are always a few in the sky on opening morning. They have one weakness as sporting quarry at this time of year. Unlike mallard, which are quick learners, pochard tend to fly round and round with sad but quite predictable consequences.

Tufted duck are another species which are clearly extending their range in Ireland. Not long ago, like pochard, we would rarely see one until well into the winter. Now they have become regular breeders in this area and numbers increase each year. One day last summer we counted nine females with their young in the bog. Not all of them remain until September but we can always expect to meet a few. Like pochard they suffer from an over-trusting nature which makes them a little too vulnerable in the early days of the season.

Two other species make spasmodic appearances here at the beginning of September. These are wigeon and gadwall. The former are more or less certainly migrants as very few breed in Ireland. Usually it is just a single immature bird that puts in an appearance. I assume that these are recent arrivals on the coast which have got separated from the family group and have strayed inland. I have only once shot an adult male in full plumage in early September.

Gadwall are the latest additions to the bog. They are not very numerous in Ireland and only a handful of wetlands hold much more than a dozen of them. They made their first appearance here two years ago. Last September one of my sons shot one on the first morning flight. Thereafter a few small packs visited the bog on and off for much of the winter. One evening I spotted four well out on the water and fired a shot to flush them. They proceeded, having circled once, to land some distance away. I repeated the exercise with similar effect and finally came away frustrated. They would not come near me, but equally they were intent upon staying in the bog.

My first preference at the start of a new season is stubble flighting, as long as I am reasonably sure that the mallard have remained faithful to the usual fields. It can happen, especially in a good year, that too many have been visiting and have cleared the split grain before August is out. Given a choice between barley stubble and wheaten stubble mallard will nearly always opt for the former. I have shot them over wheaten stubble but not that often.

My choice of stubble over bog is an unashamedly selfish one. Most of the duck enthusiasts go to the bog on opening morning. I thus have the stubbles to myself unless one of the sons decides to join me. Of its nature duck shooting is a solitary occupation and I enjoy the breaking day out of sight and sound of human kind. There is, anyway, one drawback with the bog. It is necessary to get there very early to secure a prime position. This means getting up at an even more unearthly hour. And bear in mind that later it will be a full and arduous day on the hill. It also means an exceptionally long wait until it is bright enough to shoot. Most years there are quite a lot of mallard in the bog. Greedy for another feed of barley they begin to flight out while it is still too dark to have reasonable chance of a shot. The serious shooting starts about an hour later when they have sated their appetites in the stubbles and make their return.

Mallard prefer big stubble fields to small ones and usually feed well out from the ditches. Some people build a hide. Of recent years I rarely bother. A hide can stick out like a sore thumb and the ducks are liable to give it a wide berth. If one is going to build a hide therefore, it is best to do so some days before the shooting commences so that it becomes a familiar part of the landscape. The problem with this however is that one is advertising the fact that duck are using the field. Not a good idea. One year we built a magnificent hide from a slightly broken round bale that had been left in the field. It was only constructed a couple of days before the season but, on reaching it for the first flight, we found a squatter in

Mallard on Rockwell Lake, near Cashel, in County Tipperary.

residence. The squatter refused to move and there was nearly bloodshed. Second son, who can be fiery, was with me and what the enforcers of law and order refer to as an 'incident' was only narrowly averted.

The best of the flight comes in the half light. In consequence I prefer to find a part of the field where, because of uneven ground, the operator of the combine had been forced to raise his blades. Adequate cover can be obtained by lying on one's back in these patches of high stubble. In fact one can sit up until alerted by the quacking of an approaching pack.

There are people who can sit up from a lying position and swing a shotgun smoothly at an approaching target. I have always envied these people. My technique, if such it may be called, is to wait until the pack has passed over or to the side and then sit up. In these circumstances I find the going away bird a more than reasonable target.

No small part of the attraction of all wild game for me is its lack of predictability. I watch the chosen field for a couple of evenings at the end of August to ensure that it is still being favoured. To this extent matters are entirely predictable. The mallard will come with the dawn. What is much less predictable is the manner in which they will come. In the years in which the ducks display true sporting instincts, they come in handy packs of ten or twenty and they do so at reasonable intervals. But there are other years when the entire local population decides to come in one or two enormous flocks. Two shots later the flight is over.

There is also considerable variation in relation to whether or not they deign to return after their first baptism of fire. It is hard to generalise but I find that, as long as they have grown well used to a particular field, they will usually come back despite the initial shots. Once the light comes there is no point in remaining out in the middle of the field. All one can do is seek the cover of a ditch which they are likely to cross on their return. Mallard can be extraordinarily cute. If they cross the ditch out of range they have the most infuriating habit of doing a few circuits about a gunshot and half away and then pitching out of range.

I make a point of leaving stubbles reasonably early. Hunger will eventually drive them back. Better to leave them to have a feed and restore their shattered nerves. There will be another day.

I do not know the reason but our teal packs hardly ever join their larger relatives in the stubbles. I can only recall one occasion on which I shot a teal over stubbles on 1st September. Strangely though, if hard weather descends later in the season, teal will flight regularly to stubbles, especially if the ponds are frozen.

After the first morning of stubble shooting, mallard tend to move even earlier. I suppose the extra security of total darkness has something to do with it. Usually for dawn flighting it is advisable to be in position some fifteen or twenty minutes before there is any glimmer of light in the sky. Nearly always there is a single duck which puts in a appearance, makes a circuit and then departs. Shortly afterwards the serious traffic begins. If there has been a lot of disturbance and they are really hungry, mallard can start arriving when it is still too dark to see them. I have had the experience, on more than one occasion, of lying in stubbles and hearing mallard quacking on the ground quite near me.

The sound of a large pack of mallard feeding on stubbles is quite unforgettable. They are forever on the move in search of the next delectable grain and their movement is accompanied by a range of quacking sounds and general shuffling as paddles and feathers rub against the stubble. Sometimes, for no apparent reason, mass panic sets in and they rise with a positive roar of wings. Then, realising that there is nothing to be afraid of, they descend again and the guzzling recommences.

Down in the bog the assembled will have heard the shots in the stubbles. Sound carries a long way in the stillness of the morning air. There will be four or five there for sure, and maybe a couple of late-comers. At this stage only the odd mallard or two will have been shot. A few teal, pochard or tufted will probably be down, the price they pay for simply flying around rather than departing the place when the barrage opens. Teal will even try to land again even when some of their number have been shot.

In theory the disturbance in the stubbles should redirect the mallard back to the bog. After all, many of them grew up there and it has been their home all summer. Sometimes they do return in good numbers and provide first class shooting. But, unaccountably, there are years when very few return preferring instead to seek the sanctuary of the nearby lake.

Should they decide to come back to the bog many are saved by the fact that everyone is a little too eager at the start of the season. The typical scenario is a flight of ten or twenty circling in over a high ditch. Someone fires too soon. Maybe a mallard crumples, the rest rear up to the heavens and depart followed by a hopeful fusillade of shots. As the morning progresses most will have to leave and go about their daily business. To modify an old expression, work is the curse of the shooting classes.

For those who can remain there will be more shooting. The mallard will come back eventually and it is largely a matter of perseverance. As with all game shooting, concentration is the key. As the intervals between returning packs grow longer it is all too easy to let the mind wander. Then, before one realises it, a sizeable pack has glided in within easy range and the ducks are swimming contentedly around on the water, safely out of gunshot.

I rarely get a big bag when flighting stubbles for the first time. The main reason is that the fields are very big and there is a large element of luck as to whether the mallard pass in range. Three or four would be a satisfactory outcome, half a dozen would be very satisfactory.

Next on the agenda is a flying visit to a few ponds before meeting up with the grouse shooting team. The history of ponds in Ireland is a chequered one. In former times they were abundant. Now they have all but disappeared from parts of the country. Two factors are responsible for their disappearance. Accession to the then EEC resulted in massive agricultural expansion and every rood of land became precious. Ponds took up space and therefore had to go. There were even lucrative grants available for reclamation work.

At the same time rural water schemes were being constructed and the immediate consequence was that an 80 gallon tank replaced an often sizable pond. But from locality to locality the story could be very different. In one place ponds became the equivalent of endangered species, in another many were left untouched. We are very fortunate in this immediate area as there are still a good number of ponds.

Mallard and teal can and will visit any pond but they have their definite preference. Some, often the more secluded ones, are used primarily for roosting. Others are visited mainly at dusk for feeding. In these latter ones the ducks depart at or soon after dawn and a few floating feathers or some torn pond weed are the only evidence of a nocturnal visitation.

While we are waiting in bog or stubbles others will be paying their respects to the new season on the river bank. On broad rivers like the Shannon the first shots of the morning are likely to put a lot of birds on the wing. Family parties often join up so that there can be a number of good-sized packs in the sky. Some flight them from a boat moored in the reeds, others will have made an early journey to a small island. It is legitimate to shoot from a boat as long as the engine is not running. As the shooting intensifies, the packs fly up and down the river in search of refuge. Unaccustomed to this level of disturbance the duck are probably a bit disorientated and, in consequence, tend to linger in the danger zone rather than seeking the safety of open water. Eventually they get the message. On stretches of the Shannon there will probably be some tufted duck on the move as well.

On smaller rivers there is unlikely to be much of a flight at dawn. Instead therefore, the best results are obtained by walking up the duck, if possible with a gun on each bank. Rivers are usually low at this time of year and weedy sand banks are a common sight. These are the places to find the mallard. They use the sand banks for loafing and dabble in the surrounding shallow water. As is the case with feeding ponds, freshly moulted feathers are a tell-tale sign. Local knowledge is all-important. Every river has its favoured stretches and the secret is to know the best line of approach. Many a river bank is screened by a dense growth of alder and there may be only a few spots where it is possible to get a shot. There is nothing more infuriating than hearing the splashing and quacking of departing duck and not being able to see them. Where the river bank is bare, two of us operate by walking some twenty or thirty yards back from the edge and looping in alternately. Sometimes, if there is a bend in the river one of us circles to a point just above the bend. The other person then walks the banks. More often than not mallard, on being flushed, follow the course of the river, at least for the first hundred yards or so.

In areas in which ponds are scarce, duck can be very vulnerable on small rivers in the early part of the season. In the absence of alternative waters they are left with no option but to fly up and down the river in response to disturbance. For this reason every attempt should be made to appoint some pond as a sanctuary and feed it well to attract and hold the duck.

For many shooters the season does not open until evening flight on 1st September. Pressure

A good morning in the bog. The light has come and the flight is coming to an end.

of business or a dislike of early rising, a common malady of modern man, prevent them from going out in the early morning. Other than when pheasant shooting begins on 1st November, there is probably no day in the shooting year when as many hunters are in the field at one time.

Evening flight is always a special event. There is the anticipation of things to come, the first stirring of the creatures of the night and the sense of peace that comes with the fading day. Hope, it is said, springs eternal in the human breast. Sometimes one knows that the duck will come. The signs of regular attendance are all too obvious and there is no reason to suppose that they will change their ways. More often than not however evening flight is something of a lottery. The duck may come; equally they may not. There are those nights when, in the deepening dusk, the murmur of wings high overhead indicates that on this particular evening they have chosen to dine elsewhere.

Arriving at my chosen spot of an early September evening I frequently disturb one or two sandpipers. They are passage migrants and we only really see them at this time of year. Their preference seems to be very much for large, shallow ponds with muddy surroundings. Waiting at the water's edge one gets to know the sequence of events that proceeds the flight. Early on swallows and martins are still feeding overhead but by now the swifts have gone. A slight ripple at the edge of the reeds betrays the cautious moorhen, or water hen as we prefer to call her. Make the

63

slightest movement and she is gone. If the evening is on the clammy side the midges may be in attendance. They are rarely a major problem at this time of day. Just once or twice they have succeeded in making evening flight a misery for me. But even at their most vicious they are not in the same class as their Scottish cousins. I have known sultry Hebridean days on the hill when to stop for even a minute was to invite the unwelcome attendance of these little horrors. At the first hint of dusk that most secretive of wetland birds, the water rail, may briefly reveal itself stepping cautiously across a stretch of floating vegetation. If there are trout in the water circular ripples and the odd splash announce the fact that the evening rise is underway.

In the half light the snipe begin to move. Sometimes they are seen in the air. It is really a matter of luck if one happens to be looking in the right direction. They come in with incredible speed; and a whoosh of displaced air followed by a just-discernable plop are the usual announcement of an arrival. Hereabouts they are usually not too plentiful in September but most ponds are graced by the presence of one or two at dusk. At this time of year our local snipe spend the day in secure marshy cover. From such places they flight out to their feeding grounds a little before the duck begin to move. Careful inspection of the mud at the edge of the pond will reveal a multitude of tracks left by their long-toed feet.

Once the snipe have settled in for the night the duck, if they are coming, will not delay too long. In my experience teal move a little ahead of mallard. Later in the season they become quite vocal at dusk but in early September they tend not to announce their presence to the same degree. Depending upon the degree of disturbance earlier in the day the mallard may make a couple of precautionary circuits before opening their wings for the descent. Those that have so far escaped a serious brush with humanity may come straight in.

On the first evening there are always more people in the bog than on other occasions. As well as the dedicated, who were there before daybreak, there are those who have come because it is 1st September and, quite simply, they have always come to see in the new season. Some of them, for whom shooting is really all about pointing dogs and peasants, will not come back again until twelve months have passed.

Depending upon the amount of cloud cover, dusk comes about 9pm in this corner of Tipperary. On this first evening those in the bog will have something of a wait. The local duck will be anxious for their daily fix of barley, having been so rudely interrupted earlier in the day. At the first hint of dusk, or even before, they make for the stubbles. If there is no one there to greet them they will feed non-stop for about thirty minutes and then head for the

Left
The new flight pond, still looking a bit raw but it won't be long before the margins grass over and the weeds re-colonise. Already the water has attracted duck.

bog when the light has all but gone. Some, for some inexplicable reason, forget all about barley and head straight for the bog when dusk begins to descend.

I usually return to the stubbles for the first evening flight. It is always something of a rush. Our post-grouse-shooting dinner is a long and relaxing affair and, mellowed by the goodness of a certain product of the grain, time slips away all too quickly. Flighting stubbles at dusk is usually a more rewarding occupation than the same operation at dawn. I suppose that this is because the light is going rather than coming and this engenders a great sense of security in the duck. They rarely come in one big pack at dusk. Instead, as hunger grows, groups of varying size leave the sanctuary and head for the stubbles. The flight is relatively short-lived. By 9.30pm, or even earlier, it is all over. The only exception is when the opening day coincides with the period of the full moon. When this happens the quacking hordes may keep coming and going well into the night.

Some individuals who are both lucky and cunning have a special reason to look forward to the new season. Often by sheer accident they discover a pond which is attracting a few mallard. With the opening day still some way off they guard their secret jealously.

At a quiet time of day, when they are unlikely to be observed, these gentlemen pay the place a fleeting visit. Just long enough to scatter a few fistfuls of barley in the shallows. On the appointed day they duly reap the reward of their subterfuge and then the rest of us have to spend the next weeks hearing about what we missed.

Duck shooting has one great advantage over all other types of game bird shooting. It can be slotted into a busy lifestyle much more easily. The pursuit of pheasant, grouse and woodcock is, of its nature, time consuming and takes place during the hours of daylight. Ducks are thoroughly accommodating creatures. Assuming that one lives in a rural area they present opportunities at both ends of the day.

Once the hurly-burly of the opening day is over, most sportsmen settle into something of a routine as regards their duck shooting. This tends to involve evening flight, at least until the short days of November arrive, and walking up ponds and streams at weekends. Initially much of the shooting takes place in the tried and trusted spots. Such is human nature. Our local bog gets something of a hammering for the first few evenings but interest gradually dwindles as the mallard realise that there are quieter and safer places to live. Go down to the bog a week after the season opened and you are likely to meet no more than the odd suicidal pochard or tuftie. Much the same holds for the stubbles. Duck quickly lose interest in a feeding area that comes under any serious degree of disturbance. I find that a good barley stubble will generally provide a couple of flights. In an ideal world a site, once shot, whether it be a wetland or stubbles should be left for the very minimum of a week. Unfortunately our shooting regime is not really compatible with this. Different individuals go out on different evenings. I could find a pond which is flighting well, shoot a few birds and then vow to give it a good rest. But, unknown to me, another individual or group, having heard the shots might decide to try their luck the following evening.

Most of us have a number of favoured ponds. In the course of the season each of them will deliver at some stage. There will also be, assuredly, plenty of blank nights as well. In my younger days I had two superb ponds all to myself. These were the last of a chain of ponds that had been developed for the pleasure of a landlord of old. The chain stretched over the best part of three miles and all the original ponds were located on rough grazing ground where mountain and valley meet. I think that there were, originally, eight of them but the rest had been drained in the Forties and Fifties as a prelude to tree planting. I would never have known about these ponds had it not been for a chance meeting in a pub with a very old man. It transpired that he had been a gamekeeper many years before. When he discovered that I was interested in shooting he told me about the ponds and volunteered to show me them the following day. He was as good as his word and despite his years he was still able to travel the rough ground. Sadly he died only months after our meeting. One of the ponds, the better of the two as it later transpired, was quite small. It was surrounded on three sides by slightly raised heather-covered banks. The fourth side was low and merged into a wet and rushy area which could be quite treacherous on a black night. At one end of the pond an old and misshapen Scots pine provided the only cover anywhere near the water.

Conventional wisdom suggests that the best ponds lie over limestone, the alkaline conditions nurturing a much greater diversity of plant life than is found in ponds on acid peaty soils. These two ponds defied conventional wisdom. In and around each of them vegetation could only be described as luxuriant. They were at their best for mallard in September. Unbelievable as it may seem it was never necessary to check them for occupancy in the latter days of August. Turn up in good time on the evening of 1st September and the ducks would always oblige.

There were years when the mallard packs came in so close behind one another that the latest arrivals would be pitching on the water before one had time to send out the dogs to retrieve the fallen. When the old gamekeeper first showed me the ponds he told me about his earliest memories of duck flighting along the fringes of the mountains. It was his job, as a very young boy, to hold two ponies some half mile away from a pond on the evening of a shoot. Each pony had two panniers slung across its back. When the shooting was over and the ducks gathered he would bring the ponies up to take them away. These were all genuinely wild mallard. So plentiful were duck that no one ever thought about rearing and releasing. I thought at first that my old acquaintance was exaggerating. However, considering the numbers of ducks that came when I started shooting those ponds over sixty years later I quickly realised that he was not.

All good things they say come to an end. In the late 1980s every piece of rough ground was being snapped up for forestry. Having minimal grazing potential this particular place, some twenty five acres, sold for

RIGHT
A September mallard from the stubbles.

the princely sum of £5,000. It is now a spruce jungle. A few years ago I broke through with no little difficulty to where I thought the pond had been. All that was left was a slight depression in the ground and a few tussocks of rushes.

The other pond was much bigger and it was totally exposed. All we could do at dusk was crouch down and keep very still on hearing a distant quack or the music of wings in the sky. Long ago, apparently, the gamekeepers were ordered to set up temporary hides about ten days before a shoot. For some reason their lord and master did not want the landscape sullied by any permanent construction.

I was at this pond one evening in early September accompanied by a cousin. The same man had little interest in shooting, other than blowing crows and pigeons out of his corn, but had decided to come with me probably because he had nothing else to do. It was the beginning and end of a shooting partnership.

This pond was the last in line of the original chain and duck would normally come in from the south west, easily visible in the after-glow of the setting sun. On this particular evening is was still quite bright but in the distant sky there were a number of promising dark smudges slowly growing larger. Each smudge was a satisfactory bundle of mallard. There was no question but that they had our pond in mind. Then, as so often happens at evening flight, a single duck appeared overhead and started to circle. It was still way out of range when my soon to be ex-shooting partner saluted it with two barrels. The rest is history. The duck flew away unscathed and the smudges which had come fairly close wobbled and faded from sight. End of that particular evening flight.

The story of this pond has a happy ending. The land on which it is located came into the possession of a kind and generous sportsman. He gave it to the local gun club as a sanctuary. In later years more ponds were dug out. With the cessation of grazing, once the land had been fenced off, trees and shrubs began to take root and it is now a place of solitude and great beauty. Willows, silver birches, alders and all other trees that thrive on damp ground are there in profusion. Several broods of mallard are brought out on the ponds every year and in winter, teal and mallard abound. Only two weeks ago we unveiled a memorial stone on site to honour those first club members who had the foresight and energy to develop the sanctuary. It is places like this which will ensure sport for the generations to come.

Far out in the mountains are two other watery places. One is a boggy stream that widens at intervals to form what can just be described as ponds. There are three of these, each only ten or fifteen yards from the next. Two are shallow and apt to dry up during periods of drought. The third is deep and treacherous; I once saw the bleached skull of a mountain sheep protruding from the surface. The other place is an ancient corrie lake, covering a little more than half an acre, which lies hidden at the foot of a steep and stony mountain. Except for a small outlet which sends water babbling and cascading down to the valley it is surrounded by high ground and rarely sees the sun. I think that it is filled with the coldest water that I have ever came across. Once, and never again, we decided to cool off with a swim on a boiling August day. It was the shortest swim that I ever took. We came out gasping for breath at the sheer coldness and blue at the extremities. I can only assume that the lake is fed by springs that lie deep in the bowels of the earth.

We discovered the stream with its three ponds whilst grouse shooting one evening. The adjoining rushy ground suggested that there might be a snipe or two around. To our amazement a mallard rose when we approached. It had hardly been retrieved when another one swept in without circling and paid the supreme price for failing to see us. Feathers on the upper of the three ponds indicated that it was in regular use. A few evenings later we returned to see if there would be an evening flight. Mallard did come in, not in great numbers, and we shot two or three. Since then we shoot the ponds a couple of times each season. They are at their best in September and few ducks go out to them after the middle of

Golden plover and snipe, the produce of the October heather bog.

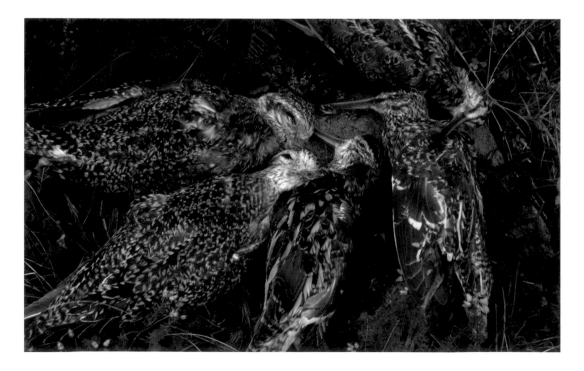

68

October. The remoteness of these ponds is a problem when returning to the car after flight. It is over a mile and on a dark night the journey can be a hazardous one. Walking mountainous ground by day is tough enough, at night rocks, clumps of heather and every other sort of impediment conspire to make life as difficult as possible. This is a place where one is all but assured of a pair of mallard but teal rarely go there. I can recall only one occasion on which we shot a teal. Down the years the best flight yielded eleven birds, we were delighted with this success until it came to humping them back to the car. Good mallard weigh around 2½ to 3 pounds and, whilst their combined weight of something over two stone may not seem much, we were more than pleased to get back to the road that night.

Twice, while settling in to await the duck, I have witnessed a sight which I have never seen elsewhere. On each occasion a cock grouse crowed just as the light was about to fade and then proceeded to flight across the ponds to the adjoining marshy ground. He was followed the first time by two single birds. On the second occasion three more grouse flew to the rushes. The surrounding mountainside is fairly arid and I presume that these evening flights were inspired by the need to obtain water.

I had passed the corrie lake many times in the course of grouse shooting expeditions. Never once had I seen duck there or, for that matter, any indications that duck were using it. It is a dark and inhospitable place. Then, one late September morning I noticed a mallard flying towards the lake. I made my way across the heather and, as I drew near, the sheer volume of quacking indicated that the mallard had plenty of companions.

The only approach was to walk up the stream to the outlet point. This was a comparatively simple exercise because the bed of the stream fell sharply and there was high heather on both banks. I was able to make the edge of the lake without being seen. When I stood up, over fifty mallard rose, nearly all of them in range, and I shot a pair. From the amount of feathers strewn around the banks it was clear that the duck had been using the place for some time.

Not long afterwards I happened to mention the incident to a friend. He was intrigued at the thought of shooting duck at the lake and suggested that we try an evening flight there. Without giving the matter much thought I agreed. It was into the second week of October before we could find a mutually convenient evening. On the appointed day we parked the car at around 6.30pm and set off for the lake. At that time of year dusk falls before eight and we had to cover the best part of three miles across some very rugged country. Arriving at the lake we discovered that the omens were not promising. No duck there and no indications of any recent presence. Disheartened we sat down and waited. And waited and waited. By nine it was almost pitch dark and long past time to depart. It was then that I realised just how ill-advised the mission had been.

Our journey back to the car is one that I will never forget. For starters we only had a rough idea where the car was. Stumbling and falling in the darkness we made incredibly slow progress in what we hoped was the right direction. Our only salvation was the very occasional light from a distant passing car. It took us more than two painful hours to get back. I have never tried to flight that lake since. What is more I have no ambition whatsoever to try again.

As the days of September slip away, the duck shooting becomes increasingly patchy. We are still heavily reliant on local birds and they have grown well used to the ways of man. They spend their days in sanctuaries or on quiet waters where they are not disturbed. At dusk they flight to their feeding ground as ever; the secret is to find these feeding grounds. The usual ones have been deserted and will see little duck until later in the winter. Stubbles are still visited. Now it is the turn of the spring barley ground. Winter barley stubbles, if not already under the plough, will not survive any longer. By early October the green shoots of next season's crop will have emerged. If the stubbles were left solely to the duck there would probably be sufficient grain to last well into November. But as the frosts come and the countryside grows hungry, rooks and pigeons descend in their hundreds and vacuum up what is left.

The first migrants will have touched down on the bays and mudflats around the coasts but few of them will venture inland just yet. Unless, that is, Mother Nature takes a hand. Across the Atlantic the hurricane season is well underway. Having wreaked devastation along the coastal states, some of these hurricanes, by now down-graded to mere storms, cross the ocean and provide us with the first taste of winter. Rivers that have been low all summer can swell in hours and spill into surrounding low lying fields. Just submerged grass is irresistible to wigeon and they are likely to be drawn inland in the wake of the storm. Literally overnight the well-educated local mallard are liable to throw caution to the wind in the face of fresh flooding and become uncharacteristically vulnerable again.

If global warming is the reality I now believe it to be, autumn storms will certainly become more common in Ireland. At the moment the flooding of low lying land is only an occasional phenomenon during September. The future may prove to be very different. The signs that global warming is with us are now all around. For the last three years I have picked mushrooms in our fields in the middle of June. Not that long ago no self-respecting mushroom would dream of showing itself before the end of July. The rooks too are changing their nesting habits. They are steadily relocating from the highest swaying tips of beech and ash to lower, more secure construction sites.

One of my favourite ways to spend a late September morning is to visit ponds and lonely stretches of rivers that I have not seen since the previous January. This means a Saturday morning and if the weather is right there is no more beautiful time of year. The ditches are laden with blackberries, the rowans berries shine bright orange in the early morning sun and the slightest hint of mist lingers over the fields. The bag will not be filled but along the way it would be an unlucky shooter who did not meet a few mallard and maybe a teal or two. If the duck are not to be found there is always the last of the season's mushrooms to pick. On these early morning rambles there are a couple of ponds that can be awarded five star rating. One in particular is my favourite. It is no more than twenty five yards across, circular and has a tiny island in the middle on which three ash trees grow. All around the pond are smaller ashes and lots of brambles except at one point where the ground is bare and muddy because cattle come to drink. I do not often meet mallard here but it is by far the most regular roost in the area for teal. Because of the surrounding trees the only escape routes in September, whilst the leaf is there, is straight up. I think this pond must have been the original inspiration for the springing teal. Later in the winter when the leaves are gone some of the smarter teal jink out through gaps between the branches.

Over the years I have grown cynical of agricultural initiatives from Europe. In one decade drainage and all manner of reclamation work is generously funded. In the next these very practices become the farming equivalent of serious criminal activity. One scheme, however, has my approval. This is the latest version of the Rural Environment Protection Scheme, commonly known as REPS 3. To my mind this is the first serious attempt to retain existing habitats and to develop new ones. REPS has made a significant difference to many ponds. Now that they are fenced off, vegetation is growing in the shallows and on the banks. Bare edged ponds with little to attract waterfowl have been transformed into quality feeding areas.

Before I leave September, I must make mention of another season that opens during the month. Under the provisions of the Open Seasons Order, hare become legitimate quarry on 26th September and the season extends to 28th February. To my knowledge there has never been a tradition of hare shooting in Tipperary. For that matter I know of nowhere in the country where hares are shot. And rightly so. The hare is another man's sport and I am always pleased to see a man with his coursing dogs deriving the same degree of pleasure from his sport that I do from mine. I must add a rider. In February I set a long line of silver birches parallel to a drain. A hare has barked some of them and actually felled others. Its work reminds me of film I have seen of beavers in action in North America. So far I have tolerated this creature. It should not rely

The rising of the moon. Wigeon should soon be on the wing.

71

too heavily on my future goodwill.

Only once in my life did I shoot a hare. That was during my college days in England. During the winter months we spent far more of our time than we should have in pursuit of enormous flocks of wigeon which in those days came to floodwaters of the Ouse. As the waters receded from the fields, hares would miracously appear in big numbers. I had grown friendly with an old Polish ex-army officer called Sigmund. He was a marvellous character and he had a wooden leg. Sigmund was one of those extraordinarily brave cavalry officers who tried to defend their homeland against the Blitzkreig of 1939. In the process his leg had been shot off. One evening he confided to me that he and his wife had a passion for jugged hare, something that they had not had since their escape from Poland when the red armies moved in. A few days later we were crossing a field to the last of the floodwaters when a very large hare lolloped by. Thinking of Sigmund, I shot it. I had two reasons to regret that execution. Carrying the hare for the rest of the evening was penance enough. Much worse was to follow.

In the fullness of time a friend and I plus our lady friends were invited to partake of the hare. It must have been stewing for hours. When we arrived at Sigmund's house the whole place reeked of the overwhelming smell of hare. With traditional Polish hospitality our host produced a bottle of vodka which seemed to disappear with extreme rapidity. Another bottle appeared and suffered a similar fate. I remember little more of the ensuing dinner except that we drank a lot more vodka. The evening had three repercussions. Neither the friend nor I saw the two lady friends again. We could only hazard a guess as to why. I vowed never to eat hare again and I developed a lifelong antipathy to vodka. Since that fateful evening the evil liquid has never passed my lips.

LEFT
Well met by moonlight:
a mixed bag of
wildfowl including
shoveller, wigeon,
teal and mallard.

October:
the Month of Migration

For the majority of shooting men, October is a quiet month. The best of the mallard shooting is over, at least for the time being, and pheasant shooting does not begin until 1st November. So what is there to do? If one has the inclination for it, as I most certainly have, snipe shooting after a slow start gets better and better as migrants pour into the country. But snipe shooting, surprisingly, does not have wide appeal. This is something that has always puzzled me. I can count in single figures acquaintances of mine who go out specifically for a day's snipe shooting. The great majority may shoot a few birds or there again they may not. Some will reserve their fire for those frustrating days on which other game proves too elusive. Shabby treatment for a bird which, more than any other, rarely provides anything but the most testing of shots. I can only think of two situations in which snipe can be less than challenging. During those now all-too-rare periods of extended frost they tend, like teal, to lose some of their jizz and should be granted safe passage. Newly arrived snipe, maybe on account of a long flight, sometimes appear lethargic and rise more slowly than they are usually wont to do.

There are a number of stock replies to the question, 'Why didn't you shoot that snipe?'. The most common, in my experience, is that it is 'not

ABOVE
Dawn breaking over our main flight pond.

worth a cartridge'. Highly insulting to a noble species and thoroughly undeserved. Next on the list is 'they are too small too eat.' So what? Shoot enough of them and you have the makings of a fine meal. Years ago a fellow enthusiast confided that he always cooked his snipe in a deep fat fryer. It seemed a little unorthodox when he first mentioned it but having tried this novel culinary approach I can recommend it unhesitatingly. Shooting lore from a different time held that snipe, like woodcock, should be plucked but not drawn when being prepared for the table. Those hardy men must have had strong stomachs. When the birds had been roasted the cavity was opened and the entrails shaken out on to hot buttered toast. This I could not cope with. Down the years I have, quite simply, shot too many departing snipe with bits of earthworms still in their bills. I enjoy being a carnivore but there are limits. The worst excuse for failing to fire at a snipe is that 'the shot might disturb the pheasants.' All I can say is that the gentleman quoted would be most unlikely to cause a pheasant much concern should he happen to meet one.

I think that a large part of the problem that people have with snipe shooting can be traced back to a few unfortunate encounters in their early sporting days. It is analogous to the difficulties that many people have with mathematics. Something happened when they were young, the brain decided that this thing was difficult and built up a mental block. Such blocks are easily put in place. In the case of mathematics a particular concept may have been badly explained. In the case of snipe shooting it might have been due to a string of misses in front of a companion.

The reality is that snipe shooting is not especially difficult. Like all successful wing shooting it requires good balance at the moment that

The tell-tale signs of snipe: beak-probing holes and footprints on the soft mud.

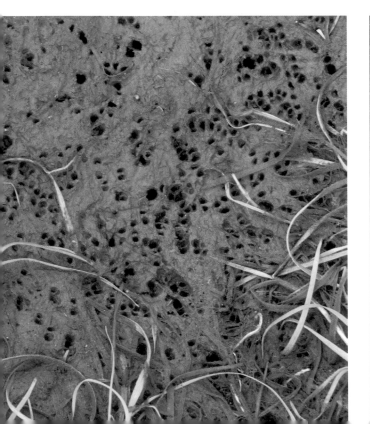

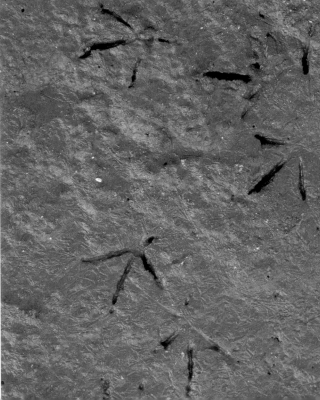

the gun is discharged. The eyes automatically follow a moving object and the brain instructs the hands to follow the eyes. But the brain cannot be expected to carry out this simple act of co-ordination if the shooter is staggering. Since most snipe shooting is over rough, boggy and tussocky ground, the only way to maintain a reasonable balance is to walk quite slowly. I have often watched a line of guns shooting a bog and it is always abundantly clear that they are moving far too quickly. One must also discipline oneself to not look down all the time. There is always a big temptation to do just this because of the fear of falling. That essential eye/hand co-ordination which results in the gun being fired at the single correct moment requires that one actually sees the bird leaving the ground. Too many people cross the bog with their eyes fixed on the ground, looking for the best place to next put the foot down. Then they look up suddenly in response to a departing bird's screech. Off-balance, the resulting shot will be wide of the mark. Unfortunately, such can be the spread of small shot that once in a while a stray pellet succeeds in downing a bird. I say unfortunately because the shooter thinks that he has pulled off a good shot and because he has learned nothing. Next time a snipe rises he will be looking down again and will in all probability miss.

Realistically one has to look down at times, but the practice must be kept to a minimum. There will be an inevitable price to pay on occasions, like falling on one's face in oozing black mud or stepping thigh deep into a drain. Been there; done that. But all sports have their hazards and if one wants to succeed one lives with them.

Tactics for Snipe Shooting

An age-old debate amongst snipe shooters is whether to walk the birds up or down wind. I have come to the conclusion that on most occasions it does not really matter. I tend to walk them upwind when I can but the reason for doing so may not bear scientific scrutiny. I think that it gives me an extra milli-second if they have to rise directly into the wind. It is probably all in my mind because just as many fall when geography dictates a downwind approach.

My preference is to leave the pointer at home when I go snipe shooting. Others, I know, derive great pleasure from working setting or pointing dogs across a good snipe bog. Each to his own. Snipe do not have to be found, like grouse and pheasants, and I enjoy the sudden and often unexpected appearance. Even though every snipe bog has its best spots there is always the glorious uncertainty. Half way to a good spot, a snipe is quite likely to rise from somewhere unexpected and the subsequent shot then clears the good spot of all its inhabitants. Our springers stay in the dog box unless required for a retrieve at the end. One cannot have it both ways. If, like us, one expects springers to tear like mini elephants into every woodcock cover, one cannot then realistically expect them to walk obediently to heel across a snipe bog. To be very honest I do not think that I have ever owned a springer that walked obediently to heel. I keep my eye on the falling bird and usually have little difficulty in recovering it. The awkward ones are those that fall in a dive, after the manner of a dart, and bury their bills in the mud in the middle of a dense clump of rushes. A successful right and left brings its own problems. Such is the intensity of the moment that I usually lose all knowledge of the whereabouts of the first bird. I am aware that it is down, otherwise my brain would not let me turn to a second target. I have exactly the same problem when two duck are down on a dark night. These are times when springers really earn their keep. That same unquenchable energy will drive them on until the bog delivers up the most well-hidden of fallen snipe.

Snipe have long since become my staple shooting diet. Like most people I started with a passion for pheasants but, as the years went by, they were downgraded in favour of snipe.

I suppose that the challenge went out of pheasant shooting, something which never happens with this lively jinking inhabitant of wild and wet places. As well as this I can go out any day once autumn is with us and be sure that I will meet snipe. And on most days a decent number of them. In contrast, often the first few weeks of the pheasant season, a lot of walking might produce a bird and then again it might not.

MIGRATION OF THE SNIPE

Whilst we rely heavily on migratory snipe for our winter sport, the resident population is not unsubstantial. Published figures suggest that there are some 25,000 to 30,000 pairs in the country. I believe this to be a considerable underestimate. Most counties, despite the land reclamation works of the 1970s, still have plenty of suitable nesting habitat. It would not surprise me if we had at least 100,000 pairs here in spring. No one knows how many migrants join the local population in autumn and winter. The number is enormous; certainly many hundreds of thousands. No game bird is more numerous in mid-winter than the snipe. As September passes the trickle of early arrivals begins to gain momentum, a momentum which causes the trickle to become a flood before October is done. Those who study bird movements claim that the main arrival takes place during November and December. I disagree. If more of these experts walked the bogs and fields and mountains they would certainly revise their views. There is no doubt in my mind that by the end of October a very substantial proportion of the wintering population has taken up residence. More will, of course, come as winter progresses. Snipe from many countries favour Ireland. They come from Iceland and the Faroe Islands, from northern Britain and Scandinavia, from the far off Baltic states and from further east. As well as this, when harsh weather settles in over the mainland of western Europe later in the season, many of the snipe wintering in these countries make a journey west in search of the milder conditions that normally prevail in Ireland.

In actual shooting terms October begins much as September ended. A typical week takes in a couple of evening flights, more in hope than expectancy, and a tour of carefully selected ponds and streams. Gradually then, the routine changes as snipe become more plentiful. The day now starts with a flying visit to the most likely haunt of mallard. It is necessary to get there early as others may well have the same idea. In this game there are no second prizes. After this the day is devoted to snipe.

Weather conditions will have a large bearing on where to go. Unless the early autumn has been wetter than normal, the rushy lowland bogs will not yet be very productive. The only water will be in the drains and the few snipe that are present will be probing along the banks. Mountainous country is therefore the most likely destination. The final grouse sorties of September may have given some indication as to the likely lie of snipe. There are essentially three habitat types in which snipe are found at height: heather bogs, rushy bogs and what I will call for a lack of a better term, rough ground. This latter covers a combination of stony areas, patches of white grass and bracken below the heather and recently felled plantations. It is only of recent years that I became aware of the snipe's liking for places from which trees were recently removed. They are without question the hardest of all places to walk. In addition to the normal debris of the mountainside there are stumps, heaps and rows of discarded branches and every other sort of impediment. Cross such a place without falling over at least once and you are dong well. But on their day these places can be very good for snipe.

Late one bitterly cold winter's evening we came out of a forest in which we had been shooting woodcock. The cars lay below us on a forestry track. To get to the track we had to

Promising snipe pasture: a stealthy approach will pay off.

travel a few hundred yards across ground on which trees had been felled the previous spring. As we progressed, snipe after snipe got up. There must have been well over one hundred of them. We got little shooting as it was difficult to see them in the fading light and a background screen of trees did not help either. But one man had a field day. Tired of walking the forest he had taken a short cut back to the cars where he was waiting for us. Inadvertently we provided him with the best show of driven snipe that he had ever seen. Most of them followed the falling ground and passed in range of him. He was still busy picking up when we finally stumbled onto the track. With more than the hint of a smirk on his face he complimented us on our beating skills.

It had been an exceptionally rough walk and we were not amused. But the last laugh was ours. The gentleman concerned had brought with him that day two newly acquired springers which had cost him the proverbial arm and leg. When the snipe had all been picked he discovered that one of the dogs was missing. At first he assumed that it was still searching for birds. But it failed to appear and no amount of whistling and calling had any effect. We were about to abandon proceedings when someone spotted the hound. There it was under the car, belly pressed to the ground and with no intention whatsoever of coming out. It had obviously been there terrified since its owner opened up on the snipe.

Though the high ground haunts of snipe differ dramatically in appearance they all have two things in common. Most important, there

is water in the vicinity. It may be in shallow pools, marshy patches or rivulets flowing down the hill. Then there is an abundance of cover, high but not too high. I find that snipe fight shy of vegetation that is very tall and dense. Presumably it gives predators too much of a chance. Earthworms, the snipe's favourite food, are scarce in these places. Peaty soils are acidic and support the most meagre of invertebrate populations. Areas where trees have been growing are sometimes an exception to this. The effect of root growth over many years is to open up the peat and make it more amenable to worms and insect larvae.

These high ground places are essentially roosting areas in which snipe spend the hours of daylight. At dusk they flight out to feeding grounds on the more fertile soils of the valleys. I have often seen them moving out in the early dusk but I have never seen them coming back in the early morning. I presume that they return while it is still dark. This is certainly the habit of their cousin, the woodcock. Driving along forest roads well before dawn it is not uncommon to pick up woodcock in the car's headlights. They are just standing on the road. Having flighted back to the forest they alight on a road or in an open clearing and then casually walk into cover.

In the course of an October day we will probably visit several different types of habitat in search of snipe. They will be mainly on plateaux and the lower flanks of mountains. All can be productive but my first ports of call are invariably the rushy areas. They are the least likely to disappoint.

It is always a basic requirement to keep the line of guns straight. It is especially important when snipe shooting. Game birds usually fly away from the line. Snipe are liable to fly in any direction, particularly high up where the wind can be gusty and variable. All too frequently snipe will curl in the air and swing back towards the line. They are flying fast, one's concentration is on the bird to the exclusion of everything else and the danger can be very real. I like to think of myself as a safe shot but on two occasions I have come within feet of disaster whilst out snipe shooting. On both occasions a bird got up in front and as it swung to one side I followed it and fired. On both occasions the bird fell at the feet of a neighbouring gun. Bad for the nerves, both the neighbour's and mine. For this reason I infinitely prefer to go snipe shooting alone. Any bird that gets up can be taken without hesitation. When there is a line of guns, a sizeable proportion of birds cannot be fired upon. Some rise between the guns, others fly down the line and most of the time one's concentration is reduced because of the need to keep aware of the exact position of other guns. It is a simple fact that we only shoot really well when we are fully relaxed.

The size of the bag can vary considerably on the high ground. The vagaries of weather and the unpredictability of the quarry dictate the number of chances. Then the competence or incompetence of the guns

determines the bag. On a good day, double figures can be achieved with relative ease. But for every good day there will be a couple more on which one's jacket pockets are sufficient to carry the bag.

Sooner or later the rains will come. One cannot reasonably expect to live at the edge of a great ocean and expect to bask in long periods of settled continental-type weather. When the rains come the lowland bogs will quickly become saturated and, in snipe terms, normal winter service will be resumed. For the time being our trips to the mountain will cease. Later in the season, with luck, we shall shoot a lot more high ground snipe. But we will not be going to the mountain just to hunt snipe. It will be woodcock time and the snipe will have to settle for being the second course. Throughout the season there will be snipe on the mountains but the general tendency is for them to spend more time in the valleys as winter progresses.

The Importance of Ireland's Bogland

My part of Tipperary lies over a long spur of limestone which extends into east Cork. The overlying soils are consequently rich and support a thriving agricultural industry despite the ever-changing nuances of the Common Agricultural Policy. Dairying and tillage are the main enterprises. Not surprisingly therefore, this is not a part of Ireland that one would tend to associate with bogland. The lowland bogs hereabouts are largely confined to hollows which, because of the topography, are not amenable to drainage other than at prohibitive cost. With one exception the local bogs are small, rarely covering more than a few acres. Their importance, in relation to snipe, lies in the fact that they provide roosting accommodation. This roosting accommodation is further extended by a number of reed fringed-ponds. One, in particular, is most extraordinary. It is no more than seventy or eighty yards in length and fifteen in width. For much of the year the free water surface is very small, so small in fact that it is most unusual to meet even a teal there. But the surrounding semi-solid ground which bears a liberal covering of rushes and other aquatic vegetation is surprisingly attractive to snipe. Approach the pond on a bad day and a dozen snipe will take to the air. On a good day four or five times that number will be present. It is no exaggeration to say that if a man wanted a couple of snipe, assuming he had the necessary skill, he could approach the pond on any given day and shoot them.

Those snipe that congregate in these wet places by day are never short of feeding grounds. Surprisingly perhaps, to those not familiar with the ways of snipe, the dairy farmer and the tillage farmer both contribute to its wellbeing.

Most dairy farms are now paddocked and the paddocks are reseeded at fairly regular intervals. This means high soil fertility and young, fast growing grass. Cows move on each day to a new paddock and, as long as the grass is not grazed tight, snipe are well provided for. So long as the cover is sufficient they will visit recently vacated paddocks in good numbers. Most years the cows go in for the winter around the end of October. There is still some grass growth at this time of year and, with an absence of disturbance, the paddocks can become even more attractive. For the novice snipe shooter there is no better place to gain confidence. Unlike the bog, the ground is flat and firm and there is no better chance to meet snipe on something like even terms. To the uninitiated it can be a revelation to walk across a dairy farm in winter and witness the number of birds that rise. A wet autumn may not suit the farmer but it brings an extra bonus to the snipe shooter. If, of necessity, the paddocks have to be closed early, growth continues and great habitat is available until the cows are turned out in spring.

Other pasture fields which have reasonable grass cover can also provide good snipe shooting in October. They become especially attractive to snipe when the roosting bogs are flooded.

Sugar beet is a crop more associated with pheasants than snipe in the shooting man's mind. It will however hold some snipe but numbers are usually low because the cover is too heavy. The snipe that are there are most likely to be found in parts of the field skipped by the drill or in which germination was poor. It is after the crop has been lifted that beet fields really come into their own. Beet ground is alkaline on account of a generous application of lime before the seed is set. Earthworms thrive under slightly alkaline conditions.

Each year the crop seems to be lifted earlier and earlier. Despite this, snipe are quick to find the rich pickings now at their disposal. Initially the heaps of leaves discarded by the harvester provide cover. But best of all, if the ground has been softened by rain, machinery leaves deep ruts and trenches that are greatly favoured by snipe. It is essential to make the most of beet ground because the conditions that allow good shooting do not last long. In times gone by, the leaves were left for a few weeks and then sheep were turned in to feed on them. This rarely happens nowadays. Given reasonable weather the modern tillage farmer will be in the field within days and the leaves will quickly disappear before the plough. Indeed it is not uncommon to see a beet field greening with winter barley before October is even half completed. Should the field be left untouched the snipe will still come but it becomes impossible to get within range.

A good day on the rushy bog.

There are few things more infuriating to the snipe addict than to enter a field and see scores of snipe disappearing in the distance.

I look forward each year to the few days on harvested beet ground. They add another dimension to snipe shooting. I fear however that the days of beet in Ireland are numbered. In fact they are numbered throughout western Europe. Sugar beet, so we are told, is an expensive and uneconomical source of sugar in comparison to sugar cane. Moreover, it is alleged, by subsidising farmers to produce beet, Europe is causing great hardship to the farmers of the Third World who rely upon sugar cane for their very survival. Sugar beet, it would seem, has only been grown in Europe since the time of the Napoleonic Wars when the concurrent unrest interrupted supplies. Now it is argued, there is no need to grow it here. I am very well aware that tillage farmers of my acquaintance are seriously worried about the future.

Stubble ground is always worth trying for snipe in October, particularly if the weather has been on the wet side. Like beet ground it is rich in soil invertebrates and can be attractive to snipe. The best places to try are small hollows in the field that caused the combine to leave high stubble. This provides a degree of cover for feeding birds.

I have little knowledge or experience of shooting driven snipe. We have tried it a few times but with very limited success. Maybe we have not got suitable ground. Or maybe our snipe are stupid and do not realise that they are supposed to fly in the direction of the standing guns. They have an unsporting tendency to fly to all points of the compass when flushed. In theory it should be a simple, military-style operation. Divide the guns into two groups, line up one half at the end of the bog and then get the other half to walk towards them. The walking guns are under strict instructions to fire only at birds breaking to the sides or going back over their heads. Trouble is, if a bird gets up and begins to fly to the side, a walking gun shoulders his gun, initially pointing to the front, and the

The first golden plovers of the season.

82

standing guns all dive for cover. The only remedy, which would not be popular with friends of mine, is to confine shooting to the standing guns.

Land of the Golden Plover

When golden plover reach Ireland in early autumn some congregate on estuaries and bays around the coast. Those that opt for the coast are likely to winter there unless driven inland in the face of stormy weather. They spend their time between the tide line and neighbouring pasture fields. On the tide line they must compete with myriads of other waders for the great wealth of tiny animals that live in the silt. Nature has been remarkably clever in ensuring that the competition is not too severe. No two species have bills of the same length. This means that different species harvest their food by probing at different levels. Golden plover, like grey plover, are short-billed and they feed on and just beneath the surface of the silt. The longer billed godwits go deeper and the curlews go deeper still.

The golden plover that we meet on the mountain in September will not stay there very long. Once the frosts come they move down to spend the winter on farmland. Here in Tipperary most of them have left the high ground by the middle of October. Unlike snipe they will not return again until winter is over. Golden plover are very much creatures of habit returning to the same fields year after year. They favour large field, often roosting in tight flocks well away from ditches. Freshly tilled land is very much to their liking because of the great variety of food that has been brought to the surface. Fields of newly sprouted winter corn are also to their liking. Golden plover do not appear to moult much at this time of year so there are rarely many feathers to betray heir roosts. However, white patches of droppings, often in great profusion, provide evidence of their attendance.

Like snipe, plover are also partial to freshly harvested beet fields. They seem to have a special liking for them after rain when there are plenty of puddles.

Unlike their brethren on the coast, golden plover wintering inland do not have to share their feeding grounds with many other species. In fact the green plover or lapwing is their only real competition. The two species are frequently seen in the same field where they may feed in mixed groups. But once disturbed they separate and fly in discrete flocks. About forty years ago the lapwing was listed as quarry but the population went into a quite sudden decline and hunting ceased. Not many years later numbers recovered but there was no real demand from the shooting community to re-open a season. The lapwing with its leisurely and rather laboured flight can hardly be described as a sporting target. There was also another reason why its restoration to quarry status was not sought. In many parts of Ireland, especially on wetter soils, liver fluke is a serious threat to livestock. Lapwings actively seek out the tiny mud snails in which fluke larvae develop. It would not therefore have been very farmer-friendly to start shooting them again.

The first indication that golden plover have returned is usually the sound of their whistling at the hour of dusk. For such small birds, their call can carry a long way. On occasions one can strain one's eye to locate a calling bird before seeing it as the merest of specks in the sky a half mile or more away.

Wintering flocks can vary enormously in size. Some may run into thousands. By extreme good fortune they come to the fields just behind our house. These are the same fields that hosted mallard when the barley stubbles were there in September. Of an average winter these can be as many as 500. Once they arrive they remain faithful to these fields until mid-November. After this they tend to come and go. Sometimes they may be gone for a fortnight

A drake safely delivered by Finn.

but hard weather seems to bring them back. If there has been a heavy frost overnight they will certainly be there next day. Flooding along the river always draws them away. In fact they get their name from the Latin word 'pluvius' meaning flood. They are especially attracted to the soft ground that is left when the flood has gone.

Golden plovers are wild and restless birds which are not easily approached. Shooting more than the odd one requires a definite strategy and more than a small slice of luck. Some days, they spend hours in the sky wheeling and diving but seemingly not wanting to land. Eventually they will come down but it requires endless patience crouched in a ditch for the chance of a right and left. There is the long-recognised practice of firing a shot to bring them down from a great height. They certainly come hurtling down as knots in response to the bang. Whether they come in range is another matter. I prefer to sit tight and wait. More often than not one will get a shot but there are those days when, having circled for an age and having come tantalizingly close on a number of occasions, they suddenly decide to go elsewhere. A cloudless winter sky full of golden plover is a glorious sight. There is every sort of formation, small packs, big packs, extended lines, chevrons, an ever-changing sea of movement.

The chance of walking up a flock on the ground is not normally very good. As one approaches, outlying birds start to walk then run towards the main body. The effect of this is to spook the whole lot and cause them to rise some way out of gun-shot. The best thing to do at this juncture is crouch down and wait. They may swing back and offer an opportunity. The best chances of making a successful approach come under two very different sets of conditions. The first of these is when the plover have just arrived and are still a little on the naive side. The second is early on a very frosty morning when the field is white and crisp. Possibly their senses are a little dulled by the cold so they take that couple of extra seconds before rising.

An alternative is to attempt to walk them up and drive them at the same time. In this case, one gun will probably have to make a long detour so that he can get behind a chosen ditch without being seen.

Towards evening, usually before the sun has completely slipped below the horizon, golden plover have a habit of flying low around the fields, often in quite small flocks. With experience one learns which fields are especially favoured. We take a field each and crouch out somewhere near the centre. It is best not to have a second gun in the field because the plover can come from any direction and one's field of fire becomes too restricted. We rarely make big bags when shooting in this manner. On the right evening a half dozen birds would represent a reasonable return.

THE RIGHT TIME TO SHOOT MALLARD

We do not shoot the released mallard on our flight pond until October. There is no real need to do so. The general area is quite well supplied with wild birds. As well as this, by refraining from shooting in the early part of the season, there is a better chance of some good flights later on. If released birds are shot in September, even sparingly, they have a tendency to disperse unless heavily fed. Feeding will certainly hold them but there is the perennial problem of fat, lethargic birds with low sporting appeal. I see no value in having a flight pond if the duck have not got the guile and flying qualities of truly wild birds. No one wants to shoot a large, brilliantly-coloured drake which rises under protest, does a half-hearted circuit at head height and tries to land again. At least I hope that no one wants to.

Another reason for delaying operations is that the wild mallard, and later teal, start to use the pond. Once the season opens on 1st September, duck are quick to find undisturbed places. If these places are also being fed they obviously become even more attractive. I find that in September, however well-schooled the released birds are, they are not quite as jumpy as the genuinely wild articles. When the pond is approached for feeding, the wild birds are in the air and gone just that fraction ahead of the residents.

Feeding is something that is in danger of being neglected once the season comes around. The powerful lures of mountain and bog eat up a lot of one's spare time. Nevertheless it is a task which must be done and I ensure that the pond is fed three times a week.

Two years ago we dug a smaller, second pond just over one hundred yards from the main one. We do not release on it but it is fed so that there is regular traffic between the two. It provides an extra stand on shooting days. There is a problem in the early part of the season in that the pond is slightly higher up and tends to become rather shallow during dry spells. Possibly because it does become shallow, teal show a preference for it. We were always conscious that following a shoot some of our ducks could go literally anywhere. For this reason a third pond was dug out earlier this year. It is a fair distance from the main pond and shots there are unlikely to disturb it. This new pond takes the shape of a horseshoe cutting into a deep weedy drain. Before turning back into our land the drain runs along the boundary taking water from both our neighbour's and our own bog. As a result the pond has a never-failing water supply.

Lest I forget to record it later on, the site where the pond now lies once nearly provided me with a right and left that had eluded me before and has done so ever since. The surrounding ground is rough and rushy and there is a scattering of furze bushes. When I was approaching a clump of this furze one frosty evening, a snipe got up and, at my shot, fell into the furze. As it hit the top of the bush it disturbed a woodcock from the ground beneath. The woodcock shot out and fell to my second barrel. Persons more learned than I in these matters tell me that one can only claim a right and left if the two birds are in the air together. My snipe was probably still falling when I shot the woodcock. There again it might have hit the ground before the woodcock received the dubious benefit of a charge of number seven shot. Hence my 'very nearly provided me with a right and left'.

As I type these lines of a bright May evening I am having serious reservations concerning the eventual use of this new pond. At this time of year mallard drakes fly around in packs whilst their partners are left to incubate their eggs and rear the resulting brood. My sons tell me that, when they are down at the back of the farm in the evening, they see these drake packs using this latest pond to the exclusion of the other two. On one recent evening, twenty five went in at dusk. There will be very little point in leaving the pond as a refuge this coming autumn if all our ducks decide to fly down to it when shooting starts. I have a feeling that we will have to put a gun there on shooting evenings. I also have a feeling that he will get the best of the shooting.

The First Duck Shoot

The first shoot of the season is always a special event. A few friends have been invited and there is always a certain degree of trepidation. Will everything go according to plan? We like to start this baptism of fire early and finish early so that the duck will return for the night. It is a gross mistake to go on shooting in the dark as disorientated duck can go literally anywhere.

We start with a drive a good twenty minutes before the beginning of dusk. With reasonably careful management it is possible to get the duck to fly in the required direction. In theory quite a lot should fall. In practice it is usual for only three or four to go down and an inevitable one tailing off into the distance. This will give the springers a certain amount of hard graft later in the evening. The problem is that the guns, despite being competent shots, are not used to a large number of ducks coming straight at them. Most people have no problem with a single on-coming bird and picking a pair from a small pack is not too demanding a matter. But when a hundred or more are on the wing it is all too easy for panic to set in with disastrous consequences. It is something of which we can all be guilty. It happened to me once with scaup, a species I only shoot once or twice a year, far from Tipperary. One wild January morning I was flighting duck from the cover of a sea wall. A storm the previous night had driven a lot of duck inland. Not long after daybreak the wind eased and the duck began to head out to sea. At one point I could see three

substantial waves of scaup heading straight for me, no more than 70 or 80 yards between each wave. Scaup are big and slightly clumsy duck which tend to fly straight, even when shots are being fired. I should have had six floating on the sea. If, that is, I had kept a cool head. The drill was simple. Shoot two from the first wave, reload quickly and repeat with the second wave. Then same again. To cut a long story short I panicked and, between fumbling for cartridges and trying to reload quickly, succeeded in knocking only three. Years later I can still see those big black and white packs in the air and kick myself for messing up a once-in-a-lifetime opportunity.

After the first volley of shots the massed ranks of driven mallard break up into groups which scatter all over the sky. This is a time to be a little discerning. Some of the duck, totally disorientated by this sudden and massive disturbance, will try to return to the pond. They present too easy a shot and should be given quarter. There are plenty of much more able performers to deal with. The temptation to shoot too many must also be resisted. Duck, however well released, present far too many chances at an opening shoot. I work on the principle that if everyone gets four or five birds that is more than sufficient. Ideally the shooting should stop whilst there is still some light in the sky. We aim to pick up as quickly as possible, scatter some feed on the island and give the survivors time to return before it gets really dark.

This first shoot usually takes place on an early October day. The pond is then fed daily for three or four days to restore badly shattered confidence. Thereafter we revert to feeding two or three times a week. At least a fortnight is then left before the next shoot. The format is the same second time round. We start off with a drive. There will still be a lot of duck to unnerve the guns. There is also the problem that when the first shot is fired, the duck now flair in all directions. At that very moment some of the guns will have picked a bird and be in the very act of firing. The result is that a lot of lead whistles some feet beneath its intended target.

This time the duck are unlikely to be quite as trusting as they were on the evening of the opening shot. Some will temporarily depart, others will go high and make circuit after circuit, keeping well out of range. After what seems like an eternity, and providing that the guns hiding in the reeds keep their faces down, they will eventually make the final landing circuit.

Following this the shooting is likely to slacken off until the duck begin to return at dusk. Once again we like to end proceedings early rather than late. It is hard to tear oneself away from a pond in the middle of a good flight but it is necessary in the interests of future sport.

Subsequent flights are effectively the same as those of wild mallard now that they have learned the ropes. Once flushed they will not return until dusk. From now on we disturb them in the early afternoon of a shooting day. If we left it until evening it could be very dark before they return.

Teal come and go. We never seem to shoot more than a handful at evening flight even though there are days when a lot of them lift when we go down to feed the pond. Other species drop in occasionally, shoveler in particular, but only in ones and twos. Because the pond is in a low lying area there are always snipe about. They start to fly before the duck and we usually get a few shots as they pass by. Towards the end of the season there is often a build up of jack snipe in our bog. They also fly at dusk and I have shot several at the pond fully believing them to be their larger cousins. Despite the difference in size the two birds are virtually indistinguishable against a darkening sky, except at very close range.

Once the rains come, and with them the inevitable flooding, we face something of a dilemma in relation to shooting the pond. So great is the mallard's love of dabbling in shallow flood-water that they are liable to ignore our generous scattering of barley. Of a winter's

evening it can become something of a lottery as to whether there will be a flight at all. In consequence we can only settle for second best and walk up the pond from the four sides. More teal invariably get shot on these occasions than is the case when flighting.

By mid-winter there are several hundred thousand wild duck in Ireland. The great majority of these are migratory. Traditionally, ten species have been hunted. Mallard, teal and wigeon, by virtue of their large numbers, bear the brunt of shooting pressure. The others are pintail, shoveler, gadwall, pochard, tufted duck, goldeneye and scaup. Very recently an eleventh species, the ruddy duck, has been added to the list.

A feature of duck migration is that the actual migratory flight is only rarely observed. In my own case I have seen great flights of wild geese on migration but I can only recall one occasion on which I witnessed what was clearly an immigration of ducks. There is a gap in the Knockmealdown mountains which separate the counties of Tipperary and Waterford. I have driven along the road through this gap on countless occasions at all seasons and at all times of the day. With one exception I have never seen so much as a single duck in the sky while making this journey.

Whistling of the Wigeon

The exception was one early November morning. Dawn had not long arrived and it was a grey blustery day. In the far distance, coming from the direction of the sea, I saw what looked like a small black cloud heading for the gap in the mountains. As it drew nearer the cloud was clearly a very high flying flock of birds. They were many hundreds of yards up and it was not until they passed almost directly overhead, that their outstretched necks betrayed their identity.

Because they appeared so small I could not tell whether they were wigeon or teal. Within minutes several more flocks passed over equally high. I would never have known what they were except for the fact that, for a few brief seconds, the blustery wind eased and the faintest whistling of wigeon filtered down to me.

I am told that the reason we rarely see duck on migration is because in addition to flying very high, they move mainly at night. The only real chance of seeing them, other than by a chance encounter like mine, is to wait at a likely arrival point when they may be seen as they lose altitude. I presume the best opportunities present themselves at headlands or at the edge of an estuary where it meets the open sea.

In spring we are often aware of their imminent departure because some species congregate in great numbers at traditional sites. Teal, in particular, form flocks numbered in thousands as a prelude to leaving the country.

Anyone who has waited for wigeon or teal of a winter's evening will be aware that they are very vocal in flight. The piping of teal or whistling of wigeon is often the first indication that there are birds on the way. The experts tell us that this communication helps to keep the pack together and, probably, provides a life-line for those that may have strayed. If they communicate so regularly during the winter months as they move back and forth between their roosting and feeding grounds, I presume they do so to an even greater extent during migration. It would seem logical that there is a much greater need to keep the pack together on a journey of hundreds or thousands of miles than on local comings and goings. My own experience that November morning would suggest that they remain in almost constant communication.

August sees the first of our visiting wildfowl. Then, during September, a steady increase takes place around the coast. It is however not until October that a serious influx occurs. Arrivals will continue through November and December. Most of these birds will remain in Ireland until the following spring.

Wildfowl wintering in Ireland come from a wide belt of the high latitudes of the Northern hemisphere. At one extreme they come from Arctic Canada, at the other from the far reaches of Siberia. Ringing has been vital in determining their origins. But many more young birds need to be ringed. Presently we are too reliant upon the ringing of adult birds as they pass through western Europe, in particular Holland. There are clearly practical difficulties involved because ducklings leave the nest almost immediately after hatching.

Whilst I fully accept the necessity of ringing young birds I have some reservation about the practice. These reservations stem from my visits to the Saltee Islands off the coast of County Wexford. Countless seabirds nest on these lovely islands. Some years ago whilst walking along a shingle beach I noticed a leg ring. On bending to pick it up I saw others lying between the pebbles. Since then I have always made a point if searching for rings and I usually find quite a lot. I assume that they had been fitted to young gulls at the nest. It may just be that, as with all species, young gulls suffer ferocious mortality levels. Somehow though I wonder about this as there are no ground-predators on the islands to my knowledge. I think that I would like someone to convince me that ringing young birds is in no way detrimental to their future wellbeing.

The movement of a certain young mallard as indicated by ringing has always been a source of great amusement to me. Very many years ago, before commercial production of mallard ducklings began in Ireland, duck were only reared on a small number of shoots. At the time I was friendly with a young man whose father was extremely wealthy and ran his own substantial shoot. In the course of conversation I happened to mention that I would like to lay my hands on some mallard ducklings to stock a small nearby lake. This conversation must have taken place in April or May and I had forgotten about it. Then some time in July I received a phone call from my friend asking if I was still interested in getting mallard. Naturally I replied in the affirmative and indicated that I would be only too happy to come and collect them. The shoot in question was located not very far south of Dublin. He told me that this would not

RIGHT
A mallard drake in full (as opposed to eclipse) plumage.

LEFT
'Pats' O'Halloran and son, Anthony, trying to decide who shot the mallard.

be necessary and that his father would organise delivery on a certain day the following week. On the appointed day the mallard duckling arrived, some sixty of them. And they arrived in style. I do not believe that any ducks ever travelled in greater comfort. On answering my door bell I was confronted by the magnificent sight of a chauffeur in full uniform, complete with peaked cap. Behind him was a gleaming Mercedes, the biggest that I had ever seen. The ducklings were in three picnic hampers on the back seat. These hampers were of a quality that would have graced any royal picnic.

The young mallard were about five weeks old. Because, I suppose, we had never had any before, we gave them extra special care and attention. Eventually they were released onto the lake. Wild mallard had always visited this lake and they soon began to join the released ones when they were fed. Around the beginning of October we decided to have a shoot and a number of friends were invited. At the end of the evening everyone went off with two or three birds. Later in the season one of our friends who had been at the duck shoot came down again to shoot pheasants. He brought with him a small document about which he was quite excited. It recorded the movement of a mallard since it had been ringed as a small duckling. Apparently when our friend got home from the shoot he discovered that one of his birds had a ring on its leg. The other one, presumably a wild bird, had not. Never having come across a ringed bird before, and not realising that the ones that we had been given were all ringed before coming to us, he sent it off to the address indicated. Back came the essential information. The duck had been ringed at the shoot near Dublin and later flew 74 miles south west to where it was recovered. Little did the ornithologists who keep all these records realise just how the duck had made that journey.

THE MIGRATION OF MALLARD

Mallard are by far the most numerous of the wild ducks that breed in Ireland. In fact it is probably true to say that more mallard breed in the country than all other species put together. Those who study migration claim that there is a quite substantial movement of mallard into Ireland from Britain and, to a lesser extent, from the continent. However they then contradict themselves by stating that by far the greater part of the mid-winter population consists of resident birds.

I have hunted mallard in many counties in all months of the season. My experience is in total conflict with those who claim a substantial immigration into Ireland. I can honestly say that I have never been aware of any upsurge in numbers as the season progresses. In fact the reverse is the case, exactly what one would expect of a resident species which is not given to excessive wandering. In the parts of Tipperary in which I do most of my shooting I would have a fairly good idea of the local populations. Whilst wigeon and teal numbers can fluctuate quite significantly according to weather conditions and disturbance levels, mallard remain remarkably consistent. What is more, even during those periods of prolonged harsh weather to which the European mainland and Britain are subjected, I have never been aware of the sudden appearance of extra mallard.

When mallard do leave their usual haunts it is mainly because of excessive levels of disturbance or because they have found an exceptionally good food source. This latter, in winter, usually means that someone is feeding heavily and drawing them in. Studies of recovered rings from mallard tend to confirm that they prefer to stay at home. The great majority of recoveries are from sites within a distance of 15 kilometres of the ringing site. It has been correctly pointed out, however, that this finding may be more to do with the life expectancy of the mallard than it has to do with their propensity to wander.

There seems to be a general consensus that mallard rarely emigrate from Ireland. There are very few records of young mallard ringed in Ireland being recovered in Britain or further afield. A few released mallard that had been ringed in Wexford were later shot in France, but it is likely that these birds joined up with some migrants passing through Ireland rather than being part of a genuine emigration. Such accidental occurrences are not that uncommon. There is the example of the Canada geese that cross the Atlantic in the company of Greenland white-fronts.

Birds may be ringed for reasons other than to study their movements. In particular, in the case of released game birds, to get an idea of the proportion of the release that end up in the bag. Some years ago I was talking to a man who ran a commercial duck shoot. Initially he had been ringing all his young birds before putting them in the release pens. He had stopped this practice and I was intrigued to know why. He had two

New arrivals: wigeon joining swans on the coast.

reasons. The first was that his clients felt that, rightly or wrongly, the whole thing was a little bit artificial when it became apparent that they were shooting mainly released birds. Probably all in the mind. The second reason was that the same clients were typically unwilling to disclose how many ringed birds they had shot. Presumably because they had shot more than their allocation.

Whilst there can be little doubt that the mid-winter mallard population is mainly resident and sedentary, the reverse is true of teal. At least ninety percent are migratory. Living inland (the nearest coastal point to us is some fifty miles) we are not really aware of the early arrivals in August and September. October is different. The ponds and streams from which we shoot teal begin to deliver the goods. The precise time of the month is subject to some variation. This is frequently the time of year when the water table is at its lowest. But as soon as the pond starts to fill, the teal begin to appear.

Teal come to Ireland from many countries. The Baltic States and Scandinavia provide the greatest numbers but there is also immigration from Iceland, Britain and the Low Countries. It is claimed that on the east coast numbers continue to build during November and December. On the south coast is would seem that there is a decline following a mid-autumn peak. It has been suggested that this is because the birds pass on to France and Spain. I am not convinced of this. To my knowledge few teal have been ringed in Ireland and without recoveries one can only theorize as to their fate. Far more likely, in my estimation, is that they filter inland to countless small wetlands in the counties of Munster.

In the 1970s it was believed that the mid-winter population lay in the range 30,000 – 50,000. More recently this has been revised upwards to at least 50,000. Even this figure is too low. Teal are only really counted on wetlands where there are fairly substantial concentrations. But for every large pack there are dozens and dozens of smaller ones in every county. There is no doubt in my mind that the true wintering population is at least three times greater than published figures suggest.

Of all the wildfowl, teal are the most susceptible to harsh weather.

A pair of gadwall on Marlfield Lake, Clonmel. The species appears to be expanding its range in Ireland.

It is well recognised that prolonged periods of cold weather in Europe precipitate a westward movement into Britain and on to Ireland. But as quickly as they appear under such conditions they can be gone again in days if the weather moderates.

The return to the breeding grounds can start as early as January. Some years, especially if the second half of that month is mild, we see a big drop in numbers at that time. A lot of the usual haunts may be deserted by February. Unless we get a late bout of severe weather most are gone well before the end of March.

THE ARRIVAL OF THE WIGEON

During the winter months the wigeon is the most numerous of all the wild ducks found in Ireland. The population is estimated to be of the order of 150,000. Despite this abundance the average person probably never sees a wigeon, or if he does it is doubtful as to whether he could identify it. Everyone knows the ubiquitous mallard. Ponds, streams, rivers, there will usually be a few mallard in residence, be it town or country. To a lesser extent the same is true of teal though they are much less taken by urban life than are mallard. Wigeon are very different. Their ideal is a broad expanse of preferably shallow water, usually at least an acre or so. They will use ponds but only infrequently. I doubt that I meet wigeon on a pond more than once or twice in the entire season. Under normal conditions even rivers have little attraction for them unless they are very broad or very undisturbed. Inland they tend to confine their use of moving water to periods of hard frost when their normal feeding and roosting grounds are frozen over.

Wigeon begin to arrive in Ireland slightly later than teal. Very few reach our shores before the end of August. Even in September numbers are usually not that high except, perhaps, at a limited number of coastal locations. I have only once ever come across wigeon in August and that was under the most unlikely of circumstances. Towards the middle of the month I was stretched on a beach in County Wexford on a brilliant sunny day. Nothing was further from my mind than wild ducks when, out of the blue, that familiar sound to wildfowlers, the whistling of a drake wigeon, came drifting across the sea. And there he was, sailing along against a cloudless sky not many feet above the waves. It was probably one of the very first arrivals of the year though, possibly, it could have been a pricked bird that had been unable to return to the breeding grounds the previous spring. On a few occasions I have come across a wigeon in May and have always assumed that such birds are carrying some injury which prevented them from making the long journey home. They are unlikely to have been escaped birds as, to my knowledge, there are no wildfowl collections anywhere near here.

Wigeon come to Ireland from widely separated breeding grounds. Very substantial numbers come from Iceland. In fact it is generally recognised that Ireland represents an important wintering area for Icelandic birds. Other wigeon come from Scandinavian countries and from as far as Siberia. Very few breed here. We are probably talking about no more than the odd pair or two in any one year.

By the end of October large numbers of wigeon are present at most of the usual coastal sites. They are however much slower than teal to forsake these sites and move inland. It is usually well into November, or even December, before they make their presence felt in the area. This is because of their rather different habitat requirements. Teal will move inland as soon as the smallest of wetlands start to hold water. It is not really until the rivers burst their banks or the water table rises to fill the western turloughs that wigeon are drawn inland in substantial numbers.

In my experience two duck species are particularly vulnerable when they first arrive. The wigeon is one, the gadwall is the other. Just now and again I find myself in the right place on the very day that a new batch of wigeon have decided to grace us with their presence. Mallard, young or old, depart a place at great speed in response to a volley of shots. Newly arrived wigeon, even when fired upon, are apt to circle and attempt to come in again as if they cannot really believe that there is someone so malevolent as to want to kill them.

A couple of miles from my home is a low-lying piece of land that is now planted with trees. It always flooded when the Suir rose in autumn and still does, so that there are patches where the trees have never taken off. After the first flood, pools of water remain for the duration of the winter. They are always worth flighting at dusk. The trees had been set for about two years when I decided to chance flight one evening at the beginning of November. The moon was just past first quarter on that particular night. For some reason that I cannot recall I did not take a dog with me. I knew that mallard were using the place as I had seen a liberal dusting of feathers on the water when I had been snipe shooting a few days earlier.

Right
St. Stephen's morning 2005. Willow was responsible for flushing and retrieving the entire bag.

Wigeon Flighting at Dusk

As the time of the full moon approaches there is an extended period of twilight as the moon, already in the sky, counteracts the growing darkness of the western sky. In the early twilight I heard the call of wigeon and almost immediately a pack was attempting to land all around me. I was still standing out in the water trying to decide where I would stand for the flight. I shot two from the pack and the remainder, maybe twenty, circled and came straight back at me. I shot one of these. Several more packs came in that evening and I ended up with a bag of eight. I managed to retrieve all but two. When I got home I gently twisted one of my son's arms so that he would go down with a dog and pick up the other two birds. Being a dutiful sort of fellow he did just that. When he got there, to his surprise a cloud of wigeon lifted off the water. I had thought that the flight was well over before I left. Clearly I got it very wrong.

I have several times seen gadwall exhibiting that same careless disregard for life and limb. As with wigeon I have shot birds from a pack only for the survivors to come round again. With gadwall I think that a pack is no more than a family party as I have never come across more than seven or eight together.

In this area only a handful of wigeon roost on our few small lakes. They prefer to rely upon the very low lying fields that, once flooded, hold water all winter. Two in particular are no-shooting areas which is probably a good thing as it means that we have a constant reservoir of birds. From these sanctuaries they flight out at dusk, even to fields from which the flood-waters have all but receded. Wigeon are avid grazers and will continue to frequent fields in which water is no longer lying.

There are usually more wigeon inland during late December and January than at any other period of the season. It is certainly the time when I shoot the greatest numbers. They are only really absent if a prolonged ferocious frost drives them prematurely back to sea. But once the season is over they do not stay around very long. Even if there is late flooding we rarely see wigeon in March.

After the big three, shoveler are our next most abundant dabbling ducks. Breeding numbers are small, probably no more than one hundred pairs in the entire country, but in autumn the population swells as migrants arrive from Iceland, Scandinavia and Russia. These migrants are early arrivals and numbers usually peak in late October or November. At this time of year there could be around 8,000 in the country. It is rare to come across big concentrations of shoveler; packs of a dozen or fewer are most common.

With the exception of one extraordinary year around 1996, we rarely see more than the odd shoveler or two until after Christmas. Tipperary shoveler are clearly unaware that they are supposed to be departing the county at this time of year. In that one extraordinary year they began to appear in October and thereafter numbers steadily increased. One of my sons and I visited the bog on the morning of Christmas Eve. Out on the water there were a lot of shoveler. We flushed them and counted 78 which proceeded to circle high above the bog. A further 30 then appeared and, amazingly, the whole assembly seemed determined to stay despite our presence. We shot four that morning, the biggest one day bag of shoveler we had ever made.

Most winters we shoot a few over flooded water meadows when flighting at dusk. There are invariably wigeon about and on almost every occasion that I shoot a shoveler I have thought it to be a wigeon until the dog delivered it to hand. Most commonly they come in singly or in pairs.

On the water, shoveler display a clumsy appearance, probably because of the disproportionately big bill. Nothing though could be further from the truth. They are every bit as agile as teal and can make height with ease when flushed. Once airborne they are swift and efficient fliers.

The drake is one of our most handsome wildfowl and the white of its plumage is a great giveaway even at long distance. Against a leaden sky the white could suggest gulls were it not for the direct nature of the shoveler's flight. Unfortunately the drake's handsome appearance is not matched by his performance on the dining table. An old fowler once told me that the best way to deal with shoveler is to boil them lightly, then roast them and finally give them to the dog. I would not quite agree to this novel culinary approach but I do make a point of giving away any shoveler that I shoot. To date none of the lucky recipients of my largesse has come back to ask for more.

I have heard it said that of all the wild duck, shoveler are the ones most easily brought down. As I shoot them almost exclusively at dusk I cannot comment with any degree of certainty but one incident in my youth lends a certain credence to the proposition. In those distant days my fire-power was restricted to a single barrelled antique which was described as semi-harmless. Semi-harmless is a complete misnomer. It had a small hammer which could easily slip off one's thumb when cocking, with consequent unnerving moments for one's companions. I was walking at the edge of floodwater one evening with some time to go before dusk when I spotted a line of duck coming straight for me. There was no cover

Two mallard on one of the flight ponds in rather more trusting mode than usual.

so I simply knelt down and the line, six or seven shoveler, passed almost overhead. I pulled on one in the middle of the line and it crumpled and fell. Within seconds another one fell and then, a few hundred yards away, a third came down. I succeeded in retrieving all three. I have always believed that two of these succumbed to single grains.

The Decline of the Pintail

Ireland has never received its fair share of pintail. This is one of the world's most numerous ducks yet relatively few have ever come to the country. Worse still, only a tiny number remain to breed. There is still more bad news for Irish fowlers. The wintering population has declined drastically over the last quarter of a century. In the 1970s the mid-winter population was estimated to be about 8,000. Now it is down to little more than 2,000. Some of the birds, probably the majority, come from Iceland. The remainder originate from Russia.

In my youth, despite a totally disproportionate amount of time spent in pursuit of wildfowl of every description, I never saw so much as a single pintail. I was twenty years of age before I shot one. And it was not in Ireland. It was the last night of the season during my last year in college and the Ouse Washes were in flood. It was a night that I shall never forget. We used to wade out in vast acreages of floodwater and stand with our backs to a convenient ditch, waiting for wigeon. In those days they would come in their thousands. On the particular night the moon was a couple of days past full and was not due to rise until about 9pm. In consequence, after dusk had fallen and a few teal had flown, we had settled down for a long wait until the rising of the moon.

The said celestial body had just broken the horizon when the most magnificent and most terrifying electric storm I had ever seen suddenly erupted. It would have been a joy to watch from the safety of a house. But standing out in water, hundreds of yards from dry land, was another matter entirely. The sky was as bright as day and all around us lightning seemed to be bouncing off the water. Discretion, so it is said, is the better part of valour. We high-tailed it to the house of a lock keeper with whom we had become friendly. An hour or so later the storm passed and as the season did not end until midnight we returned to our stands. By now the moon was well up and there were a lot of wigeon on the move. I shot what I assumed was a wigeon from a pack that passed at long range. On recovering it I discovered that it was a duck with which I was not familiar. It was my first duck pintail.

Since that far off day I usually shoot two or three a year. Always in County Wexford. The books state that pintail come to Tipperary but if they do they have been one hundred percent successful in avoiding me. Years ago it was not uncommon to meet packs of ten or twenty in Wexford; sometimes they would be in a mixed pack with wigeon. In recent years I have only come across single birds.

Great numbers of pintail congregate each winter on the estuaries of western England such as the Mersey and Ribble. What has Ireland done wrong that they steadfastly refuse to take the short journey across the sea?

Tufted duck and pochard are our two major diving ducks. The small breeding population of pochard and the much larger one of tufted duck are augmented by migrants in autumn. Pochard, in particular, are early arrivals and by September great rafts of them can be seen bobbing up and down on the waters of western lakes, especially Lough Corrib. Slightly later the tufted duck arrive, and not uncommonly the two species can be seen in mixed flocks at this time of year.

Most of our wintering pochard come from northern Europe. The origins of tufted duck are rather less certain. Considerable numbers come from England and Scotland. More come from further east, mainly Scandinavia. Wintering numbers are broadly similar for the two species. The mid-winter population of pochard is estimated to be in the region of 30,000 and for the tufted duck 25,000.

During October the big concentrations on the western and midland lakes begin to disperse. Gradually they move on to waters of sufficient depth to meet their feeding requirements. In the case of Tipperary they are slow to arrive. I normally expect a small influx of tufted duck in this area around the middle of December. The pochard follow a little later. In some years we see few migratory pochard before the last couple of weeks of January.

The other two diving duck that we hunt are scaup and goldeneye. Both are essentially birds of the sea. Scaup rarely come inland unless the weather becomes ferociously stormy. I have never seen a scaup in Tipperary. The handful that I shoot each year are ones that try to cross the sea wall when the wind is approaching force seven or eight. Unlike scaup, goldeneye do winter on inland lakes. But again, I have never seen one in Tipperary. Those that I have shot on the coast have been single birds and almost exclusively females. It is my understanding that goldeneye are one of those species in which males and females use different wintering grounds. The males, apparently, winter further south. My own bag record would tend to confirm this. Most years I shoot a few ducks but only twice have I shot a drake.

A cormorant taking advantage of an inland duck sanctuary. Note the drake gadwall in the foreground.

For most of us, diving duck constitute no more than a small part of the annual bag. In my own case a couple of dozen is as much as I would expect to shoot in any one season. But some sportsmen are lucky enough to live in places where diving duck are very plentiful and in consequence they can enjoy some very exciting shooting. I have a friend living in Northern Ireland whose home is conveniently near to Lough Neagh. This is one of Europe's greatest wildfowl lakes. Hundred of pairs of tufted duck breed there and in winter they are joined by thousands more. Very large numbers of pochard and goldeneye also winter on the lough. During September my friend gets a little mallard shooting there but, once October arrives, diving duck provide most of his sport. If there is a good wind at dawn the tufted duck provide superb shooting as they flight up and down the lough. Sometimes, he tells me, they keep on the move for several hours.

November:
the Month of the Pheasant

1st November – the biggest day in the Irish shooting calendar. Before the sky is fully bright the crackle of gunfire will announce that cock pheasants are once again fair game. For at least a few hours there will be more sportsmen out with dog and gun than on any other day. In Northern Ireland, as is the case with grouse, there is an earlier opening date. The pheasant becomes legitimate quarry on 1st October, but many sportsmen tend to allow a partial reprieve until later in the month.

Each shooting party will have laid its plans with meticulous care. They will probably head for the same place as they did the previous opening day, and the one before. Likely destinations will be beet fields, or gardens as they are called hereabouts, stubble ground or for those living away from the tillage areas, rough and rushy places with a scattering of trees and shrubs. There is a danger that some renegade has similar intentions concerning one's chosen patch so it is necessary to get there early. Mankind can be a devious animal. It is not unknown for such a devious animal to leave his car parked at the chosen spot the night before. The said renegade will then assume, should he get there first, that he has been beaten to the draw.

Ten years ago there was probably more activity on opening day. This is not to say that enthusiasm is any the less, or that there are fewer hunters of pheasants. There is every bit as much enthusiasm and there are more hunters than ever before. It is all about a sociological change. 1st November is one of the most important days in the Christian year and is a holiday of obligation. This means that it is a day on which there is an onus to attend Mass and refrain from servile work, as on a Sunday. In the not too distant past these requirements were observed without question in rural Ireland. Farmers did no more than was necessary to ensure the well being of their stock and businesses closed for the day. The shooting fraternity were conspicuous by their presence at Mass the previous evening. They were thus free to pursue that colourful alien at dawn the following day.

All that has now changed, and changed quite dramatically, with the explosive growth of the nation's economic health. Some commentators now refer to 'post-Christian' Ireland. Probably something of an exaggeration but yet not without a degree of truth. The reality is that the

Loading up for a pheasant shoot.

great majority of people now go about their usual business on 1st November as they do on any other working day. Businesses no longer close and employers expect to see their staff at the appointed hour. For the ardent pheasant shooter this means that he must confine his sport on opening day to, at best, a couple of hours (dawn comes at around 7am) before answering the call of the material world. Other than that he will have to wait for the weekend and live in the hope that at least some of his favourite places have not 'been done'.

On a still, dry morning pheasants are down from roost early. They frequently drop to earth or take off on the day's first flight whilst it is still a little on the twilight side. But if the day is wet or murky they may stay up in the trees much longer. This is why it is sometimes possible to get some shooting later in the day even though the ground has already been shot over.

As the first morning passes, the level of gunfire gradually decreases. In some cases this is due to substandard fitness levels, in other cases there are those whose annual pilgrimage is complete when there is a bird in the bag. Then there are those who must depart the magic world of the shooting field to address the business of making a living. There is also the problem, unless the preserves of the local club are very extensive, of deciding where to go next. Many a campaign plan has been thwarted by the sound of shooting from what was to have been the next port of call.

The Test of a Good Dog

Dogs too begin to feel the pace, especially if they have just put in a couple of tough hours in beet or heavy cover. Beet can be a killer for dogs. The sheer density of the crop is such as to sap the energy of even the strongest and fittest. The underlying ground is invariably soft as it never experiences the drying effects of wind and sun once the leaves are fully grown. Then there are the rabbits and the cute old cock pheasants which test the dogs' stamina by running endlessly up and down the drills and crossing to new ones. Even dogs which become battle-hardened on the mountains during September lose some of their edge during the lazy days of October when they are not required for duty.

The excitement of pheasant shooting is akin to that of grouse shooting in that adrenaline levels rise as the dogs show greater and greater interest. Finally, there is the point, and the world stands still for a few seconds. What happens next is not at all predictable. A sudden dash forward by the dog may lead to precisely nothing. Massive anti-climax. Then there is some furious snuffling, the dog dashing hither and thither trying to recover the trail. More often than not a hen takes to the air followed by another. A wily cock in a field of beet is apt to sneak away and leave the loves of his life to face the music. But on that first day of the season it will be a poor beet crop that does not finally deliver up a cock or two.

Years ago most farmers had a plot of turnips, maybe only an acre or two. They were invariable weedy and of all places the most likely to hold a few birds. I think that pheasants preferred turnips because the leaves are less dense, so providing less of an impediment to escape. It was quite a common practice to grow adjoining crops of turnips and beet. We always hunted the turnips first as the birds that were not flushed would often filter into the beet. Sadly the turnip is now a thing of the past on Irish farms. I do not recall even seeing a field of turnips for several years.

By afternoon only the young, the hardy and the really dedicated shooters are still in the field. Most of the pheasants are well scattered having probably encountered more than one shooting party in the course of the morning. An element of luck is therefore necessary if there is to be any substantial increase in the size of the bag. There will be those who have reserved a secret place for the afternoon session. They have probably spent the morning hoping and praying that no one has had the temerity to enter ahead of them. We always take a sadistic delight in finding one of these places and getting there ahead of the posse.

Our finest hour came on one such occasion. We knew that a certain gentleman had been watching a field of beet behind his house. It was a secluded area and the surrounding grassy fields gave no hint to passing sportsmen of the good things that were there. The beet could not be seen from the road and I forget how we came to know of it. Anyway, the said gentleman was enjoying a late and leisurely lunch around 2pm after a hard morning's walking. It was his intention to potter down to the beet in his own good time and shoot a few of the half dozen or so cocks that he knew to be there. As soon as we entered the field a dog pointed and in no time at all we shot four cocks and a woodcock. This was the only time that I ever saw a woodcock coming out of beet. The late luncher was a little more than put out when we made a special point of passing close to his house festooned with pheasants. I think we actually took a few more with us from the morning's sortie in order to rub a little extra salt into the wound.

Hen pheasants are not included on the Open Seasons Order. It is possible however to obtain a permit to shoot them if there is a reasonable release programme. Driven shoots and some of the larger syndicates make use of this provision. I have no problem with it. I do however have a serious problem with the fact that the same groups can obtain an extension of the shooting well into February. If Joe Soap has to stop shooting on 31st January so too, I believe, should everyone else. It seems very wrong to me that money can buy an extension to a shooting season. This is not what a republic is all about.

A Good Rule for Rough Shooters

A cocks-only policy makes extremely good sense in a regime which is essentially one of rough shooting. Especially one in which different people shoot over a wide area on different days. The gun club movement has to be commended for the discipline which it has inspired. I do not think that any more than a tiny handful turn their guns on hen pheasants. Because the cock is polygamous there will always be a reasonable supply of wild birds as long as the hens are left alone. Should they ever become legitimate quarry I believe that the consequences would be disastrous. In a few short years the wild population would plummet.

The importance of the cock pheasant to the average sportsman cannot be overstated. It is the mainstay of his shooting. At least 10% of sportsmen shoot nothing else. The findings of a gun club survey conducted by the National Association of Regional Game Councils that covered the years 1988–1992 say it all most eloquently. 159 clubs responded to the survey. They were first asked to list the major quarry species in order of importance to them. Their response was as follows: pheasant 141, duck 8, woodcock 8, grouse 2. A further eight clubs listed the pheasant as being second most important. The average number of cock pheasants shot by club members over the period of the survey was 8.3 per season. Mallard came in a poor second with an average of 3.7 per member. The figure of 8.3 cock pheasants indicates an annual bag for the period in the range 150,000–200,000. Other research has broadly confirmed this.

The cock pheasant's premier status was further confirmed by the finding that 93% of club members shoot at least one per season. It was further found that cock pheasants constituted 40% of an average annual bag. This survey was undertaken more than a decade ago. There is no doubt in my mind that if a similar survey were to be conducted today the findings would differ little.

The proportion of the pheasant bag shot in each month of the season was also examined. As would be expected the greatest numbers were shot in November and the least in January. In fact more were shot in November (58.5%) than in December (26.0%) and January (15.7%) combined. I think that these figures are indicative of the only likely outcome if the hen pheasant was added to the shooting list. There would be, initially, a concentration on cocks but, once their numbers started to dwindle, hens would bear the brunt of shooting pressure.

It is an extraordinary thought that the most successful game bird in these islands is an alien. Whilst native species have declined, most noticeably the grey partridge and the grouse, the pheasant has prospered. It may be argued that the sheer number of pheasants is only being maintained by large scale release programmes and that, should these stop, the pheasant would suffer the same misfortune as the partridge.

I fully accept that numbers would decline considerably without the annual top-up but I have no doubt that viable populations would survive in very many places. Being an aficionado of the snipe a lot of my shooting takes place well away from what would be considered ideal pheasant habitat. Moreover it takes place in areas in which, in my lifetime, there have been no releases. Yet, year after year in these wild and rushy haunts I come across and shoot pheasants. What is more I shoot them without the assistance of a dog. I have previously expressed my views on springers

Time to pack up after a hard day's tramping through woods and over moorland.

107

and snipe shooting. The pheasant is an extraordinarily resilient bird and has adapted to life in some very unlikely places.

The capacity of the pheasant to come to terms with so many new environments is unusual for an 'exotic species', the term scientists apply to creatures that have been transplanted to new countries. I can think of no other game bird that has been uprooted and then settled so successfully elsewhere.

For centuries mankind took animals and plants with him to new territories. More often than not the newcomers were unable to cope with the prevailing conditions and died out. Some introductions were accidental and simply occurred as a result of the movement of people and their belongings. The house mouse was probably one of the first mammals to accidently reach these islands. I can find no date for its appearance here. The black rat reached Britain and Ireland in the twelfth century having travelled in comfort in the baggage of returning Crusaders. The same creature is believed to have been taken to New Zealand when Captain Cook first visited that country in the 1770s. More recently air traffic has been responsible for the movement between continents of insects and other small invertebrates.

Intentional introductions were attempted for many reasons. When Europeans colonized distant lands they took familiar animals and plants with them to ensure a food supply. They also took with them some of the creatures of the chase so that they could continue to enjoy the hunt in their adopted lands. Sometimes it is not possible to decide whether the primary motivation for an introduction was for food or for sport. Introductions of deer are a case in point. The fallow deer was brought

One of the last Tipperary beet crops. The demise of beet, courtesy of the European Community, represents a sad event for both farmers and pheasant shooters.

to Ireland by the Normans. The precise date of its introduction is unknown but fallow deer appear to have become well-established here by the twelfth century.

Since the great majority of those early introductions went unrecorded it is necessary to refer to contemporary literature in order to hazard a guess as to the approximate date. If an introduction is successful people become aware of the creature and its name begins to appear more frequently in folklore and books.

Man's preoccupation with the hunt has meant that countless game bird introductions have been attempted around the world. The pheasant has settled successfully in nearly every country to which it has been taken. In addition to Ireland, Britain and many parts of Europe, there are thriving populations in the United States and New Zealand. The species was first introduced to the United States around 1730, but it was not until the 1880s that it became fully established as a breeding species in the wild. Records show that the state of Oregon was the first to officially open a pheasant shooting season. This was in 1891 and an estimated 50,000 birds were shot in that first season.

Only two other game birds have settled with any real degree of success in North America. The grey partridge was first released in grain-growing areas near Calgary, Alberta in 1908, and is now widespread in the prairie provinces and in a number of adjacent American states. The chukar partridge was first released in Illinois in 1893 and is now present in at least seven states.

A Roman Myth

For a long period of time it was believed that the first pheasants to reach Britain were brought by the Romans. This belief was based upon the finding of what were thought to be pheasant bones at the sites of a number of Roman settlements. However in the 1930s it was demonstrated conclusively that these bones belonged to domestic fowl. It is now generally accepted that there is no evidence to link the Romans to the introduction of pheasants to these islands. In consequence the Normans must be credited with the introductions. The first mention of the pheasant in Britain appeared around 1177, but these were most likely captive birds bred for the table. With the passage of time escapees and deliberate releases laid the basis of a wild population.

There is no precise record of when the species finally became established in Ireland or Britain. It is probable that it was well-established in both countries before the end of the fifteenth century. Fynes Moryson visited Ireland between 1599 and 1603 and makes reference to the pheasant. He wrote, 'such plenty of pheasants as I have known sixty served up at one feast, and abound much more with rails but partridges are somewhat scarce'. It is interesting to note this comment on the partridge made over four hundred years ago. Rails, I presume, refers to the land rail, or corncrake as it is now better known. I have never heard of anyone eating water rails. In his book *The Ark in our Midst*, R.S.R. Fitter records that in the late 1580s pheasants from Ireland were imported to Pembrokeshire in Wales for stocking purposes, further evidence that they had become common in Ireland by that time.

Pheasants are birds of the East and the first to be brought to Britain, and then on to Ireland, were from Georgia and Armenia. The cocks did not have the white neck ring which is so common in many of our present-day birds. To distinguish these first arrivals from later importations they were referred to as 'Old English' pheasants. It was not until several hundred years later that the Chinese ring-necked pheasant reached our shores. The earliest recorded date for this species in Britain is 1768 so it is reasonable to assume that it was in

Ireland soon after.

A number of other species of pheasant were also brought to Ireland. They seem to have had little difficulty in interbreeding so that the present-day population is an amalgam of many species. Green pheasants appear occasionally in the Irish countryside. They are almost certainly carrying some of the genes of the Japanese green pheasant that was first reported in Britain in 1857. It appears to have become quite common there by the 1920s. I can find no record of its initial arrival in Ireland. Whilst it may have been here for much longer I did not see one in the wild until well into the 1960s.

PHEASANT SCHEMES

In an earlier chapter I mentioned that many clubs had moved away from the use of a conventional release pen. Their annual release programmes were clearly not delivering the goods for the autumn shooting field. Ironically it was a government grant scheme aimed at improving game stocks that was to bring about a realisation of this fact. Introduced in 1961, the pompously entitled 'Native Resident Sportsman Game Development Scheme' was the catalyst that concentrated minds on the need to restock preserves. Financial support was made available for the purchase of poults, the construction of release pens and the establishment of game crops. Whilst the main thrust of the scheme was to expand pheasant numbers there was also support for such activities as the development of snipe bogs and heather moorland. The big demand for poults triggered by the scheme resulted in the establishment of a number of game farms. These too received grant aid for the purchase of incubators and other essential items of equipment.

It would be a little naive to think that this scheme was entirely altruistic. In my experience politicians do not do altruism. The essential raison d'etre of the scheme, in the view of this cynic, was to boost game bird populations to a level that could support a tourist shooting industry. Politicians of that period were anxious to find each and every means of promoting rural tourism, especially outside the main summer season.

The Native Resident Sportsman Game Development Scheme lasted for some twenty years. It finally came to an end when the economic situation deteriorated in the early 1980s. By then any lingering doubts concerning the need for a review of release procedures had been dispelled when it became apparent that clubs that had been religiously tagging poults were only rarely getting reports of tagged birds in the bag.

In response to the escalating crisis of confidence in release procedures the National Association of Regional Game Councils decided, in 1981, that a formal investigation should be undertaken. This body, which represents the interests of game shooters and is much involved in the field of conservation, is formed from the country's 28 Regional Councils. There is one of these in each county, except for Tipperary and Leitrim which each have two. Each of the councils is essentially an umbrella organisation which co-ordinates the activities of the gun clubs of the county. In some counties support is also drawn from other fieldsports bodies and rural organisations.

What was wanted was a detailed study to find out exactly what was happening to poults after they had left the release pen. All aspects of the study needed to replicate faithfully the release methodology of a typical gun club. There would be no point, for example, in conducting the research against a background of predator control more intensive than usual. The obvious centre for the project was the Faculty of Agriculture at University College, Dublin. Accordingly, negotiations were initiated with the Faculty's Department of Agricultural Zoology

Evening and the end of a good mixed day.

and it was decided to set up a three-year postgraduate studentship. This was duly advertised. Pete Robertson, a graduate of Reading University, was selected to carry out the research under the supervision of Dr. John Whelan. Now Dr. Pete Robertson, having been awarded his PhD for his work in Ireland, has made major contributions to our knowledge of game birds through his work at the Game Conservancy.

It was important that the research would be carried out over terrain similar to that of a typical gun club's preserves. Fortunately, University College Dublin owned the Lyons Estate, a large agricultural research facility located on the borders of counties Dublin and Kildare. In addition to pasture and tillage ground the estate contained a more than adequate acreage of woodland and scrub.

Over a three-year period a total of 446 poults were released. They were obtained as six-week-olds from a commercial game farm. Before being put in the release pen each poult was fitted with a leg ring and a colour-coded plastic tag. As is standard practice the primary feathers of one wing were clipped to prevent premature emergence from the pen. Poults were put in the pen in late July or early August.

Once they began to come out their fate was monitored by daily searches of a circle of radius 500 metres centred on the pen and weekly searches of a circle of 1500 metre radius.

Pete Robertson's findings made depressing reading, especially when aggregated into ten-day periods following the emergence of poults from

the release pen. He found that 48% of the poults lost their lives during the first of these ten-day periods.

During the next period 30% died, thereafter mortality levelled off at 16% for subsequent periods. Overall the remains of 259 of the 446 released poults were found in the course of searches. Of all the deaths 76% could definitely be attributed to predation. Since some birds simply disappeared without trace the true figure for loss to predators was undoubtedly much higher. Foxes were the main culprits being definitely responsible for 64% of recorded deaths. In the first year of his research Peter released 125 poults. Twelve months later he was only able to say with certainty that 5 cocks were still alive. It had quickly become apparent that the worst impressions of gun clubs were not far wide of the mark.

Another aspect of the research project was to investigate the breeding success of those released birds that had succeeded in making the transition into the wild. After all, even if survival rates of released poults was very low, there would be some compensation if the survivors made a positive contribution to the wild population.

To this end careful observations were made of the cocks and the fortunes of the hens were followed by the use of radiotelemetry. Once

100% concentration. The birds will not be long delayed.

112

again the findings were disappointing, especially during the first year in the wild. Some of the cocks were unable to take up a territory being unable to compete with wild birds. Those that did succeed in establishing a territory were found to have significantly fewer hens than their wild counterparts. When compared with wild hens the released ones came out second best in two respects. They laid smaller clutches and reared significantly smaller families. For both cocks and hens the differences with wild birds were less pronounced in their second year in the wild. However, by this time their numbers were further reduced.

In the light of these findings it is hardly surprising that some clubs decided to purchase caught up adult birds rather than poults. The cost is several times greater but the return is much better. Essentially the club is paying for the pheasant's 'training' on a driven shoot. A bird that has spent a winter in the wild successfully avoiding predators and has run several gauntlets of guns must have something going for it. Clubs that decided to persevere with time-honoured release procedures were now more clearly aware of the importance of predator control. In consequence they stepped up their offensive against foxes and other predators. The fact remains however that in the absence of full-time keeping the release of poults is, at best, a hazardous occupation.

Sunday Shooting

Once the 1st November has passed the season settles into a steady rhythm with most activity on Sunday mornings. The young and enthusiastic will be out soon after daybreak, those of more mature years may well wait for a slightly more civilised hour before commencing proceedings. Strange how countries differ. In contrast to what is the norm here, game shooting does not take place in Scotland on a Sunday. I think that there is a simple reason for the difference. In Ireland shooting is every man's sport and spare time comes mainly at weekends. Whatever about the present, when Scottish hunting traditions were developing only gentlemen of means could shoot and were free to do so on any day of the week. Whether Sunday was set aside on religious grounds or to give the game a break I do not know.

Early in the season there will be some urgent ports of call. The opening day excursions will have revealed the whereabouts of a few families of pheasants and they must be visited before anyone else finds them. Then there are the cocks that 'got away'. As well there will be the inevitable tip-offs to be checked out. One has to be very careful with these. Some are genuine. Others may be the work of a cunning rival intent upon removing the opposition as far away as possible. There is a man in a neighbouring gun club area who is remarkably consistent when it comes to giving tips. The same man is a dedicated hunter of game. Should he see a shooting party about to enter a field in which he knows that there are pheasants he will invariably come over and provide detailed instructions of how to get to a (distant) place where he saw two 'big' cocks less than an hour ago.

When I started shooting we would drive to a given point, park the car and set off across country stopping only for a few sandwiches in the middle of the day. They were rather more relaxed times. Our route would take us across many farms and through a number of well known 'gaps' in boundary ditches. Farmers just about tolerated these gaps which tended to close over with briars and other vegetation in the summer only to be opened again come November. We now live in a different age: disease control on the farm is vital and the only acceptable means of entry is via gate or style. For many years I shot with a great friend, now long since passed to his eternal reward, who had the build of a prop forward. He was a farmer himself but if the dog pointed and we were both on the same side of the ditch he would just have to remedy the situation. This meant following the ditch for the minimum distance that ensured the bird would not be disturbed and then 'make a gap'. He would quite simply tear or fall through the ditch leaving in his wake a hole that a small herd of cows could pass through. The same man always carried his cartridges in his trouser pockets. Most of these would spill out as he was making the gap so we would invariably have to go back to pick them up and do some cosmetic repairs to the ditch.

Nowadays much has changed. Few shooting parties go to one area and spend the day there. They prefer instead to drive from one likely spot to another. Part of this is a reflection of modern man's dislike of over exertion. There is more to it however. With the intensification of agriculture some farms no longer contain habitat suited to pheasants. Whereas not too many years ago there was always a chance of meeting a bird on pasture land, such places are now rarely productive. Most pheasants are to be found on or near tillage ground so it makes good sense to concentrate one's efforts in these areas.

For the first few Sundays of the season the pheasant is likely to be the sole focus of attention. No point at this stage in creating extra disturbance by shooting at other birds. There will be plenty of time for that later in the month. Indeed for a significant minority the pheasant is the *only* game bird.

From time to time there will be a crafty old cock, spurs a half-inch in length, which has somehow managed to survive season after season. Such a kind presents a special challenge. He knows his escape routes only too well and succeeds in beating the dogs with almost contemptuous ease. Not infrequently the escape route involves the banks of a rushy drain or river. At the first hint of danger he is off running and will have crossed the water before the dogs have even found the take-off point.

THE GREEN COCK PHEASANT

There was such a bird hereabouts some years ago. What made him extra special was that he was green, one of the first that we had seen in the area. We would meet him quite regularly or, to be more precise, we would see him taking off in the distance at about the same time that the dogs had just picked up the scent. Usually he would run the bank of a stream as far as the Suir and then fly to the opposite bank. Sometimes his departure would be signalled by a disdainful cackle.

Like many pheasants which learn to survive by putting a body of water between themselves and their oppressors, it was water that finally proved to be his Achilles heel. One of my sons and his friend were out one morning following heavy rain the previous day. The river had broken its banks and several hundred acres of low-lying land were submerged, including the fields on either side of the stream that leads to the river. Approaching the flood, with wigeon more in mind than pheasants, they saw the green cock take off and head out across the water, gaining height as he went. Less than half way to safety he lost his nerve, did an about turn and came crossing back over the two boys. He now occupies a place of honour in a glass case in our hall.

Those used to hunting pheasants in beet will be familiar with the cock that steadfastly refuses to fly. Up and down the drill he goes, over to the next and on again. The dog, in a frenzy of excitement stops, points and races off once more. Only when the dog's fury knows no bounds is the bird finally forced into the air. One November evening not long before dusk I came across such a customer. After an eternity, and the pointer on the verge of a nervous breakdown, the cock burst from the beet and fell to my shot. When the dog brought him

Searching the beet – tiring work for a gundog.

back to me I discovered why he had been so unwilling to leave the safety of the beet. He had only one leg. The other had long since rounded off neatly at the knee joint after, presumably, an accident in early life. The extraordinary thing was that being one-legged did not appear to be an impediment to his travels along the ground or in getting airborne. He certainly took to the air with all the gusto of a normal bird.

Some years previously I had an even more unusual experience. It all started when a neighbour asked me if I could get him a pair of mallard for a relative in Dublin. The handiest place to try was a stream just two fields away from the house. If it is not shot too often this stream has a great track record in the early morning. On the day in question, it was late October, and the ground was still white with the first frost, only a single drake obliged. Picking it up I discovered that like the cock pheasant it only had one leg. The following morning, intent upon making up the pair, I tried the stream again. Once more there was only a single drake. Unbelievably he too had only one leg. To my eternal regret I did not take a photograph of those two mallard. One had its left leg missing, the other the right. I have shot countless birds since then but never since have I shot one with less than two legs.

As November slips away and the evenings shorten the emphasis on pheasants declines a little. Not, of course, for the purists; they will continue to pursue the only 'real' game bird to season's end. But for most of us mixed shooting becomes increasingly the order of the day. By now the autumn rains will surely have raised the water table and so provided the myriad of wetland visitors with their wintering quarters. Snipe and teal in particular should arrive in big numbers. The local mallard, having had some respite over the past few weeks, are also likely to be returning to their familiar haunts.

What one is likely to meet in addition to pheasants is largely

Finn delivers a cock at the edge of the forest.

determined by the type of habitat in the area. If there is scrub or forestry the first migrant woodcock will have joined the local population. Here in Tipperary it is still a little early for the main influx but we begin to meet them with increasing regularity as winter comes in. In parts of the south-west and west, woodcock numbers build substantially at this time of year and those fortunate enough to live in such places will already be gainfully employed. There are men of my acquaintance in Cork and Kerry who shoot nothing else but woodcock and snipe. The same holds true in parts of Mayo and Galway.

Coniferous forests in this area do not hold many pheasants. This is because spruce predominates and, with the closure of the canopy there are few plants present to provide food or which harbour insect life. The pheasant is far from catholic in terms of it dietary requirements but it cannot survive on fresh air alone. Some clubs use the plantations for release purposes and hold their birds by hopper feeding. This can be reasonably successful but the fox is an ever-present threat. About twenty miles from here a commercial driven shoot has been established in what is predominately coniferous woodland on the side of a hill. The forest is rented from Coillte but local clubs shoot over some of the surrounding countryside. Needless to say they are delighted to have the shoot in the vicinity as the inevitable leakage of pheasants provides them with sport throughout the season. One club in particular was deluged with membership applications when it became apparent that its preserves were never lacking in pheasants.

116

Gun clubs are autonomous outfits and their rules concerning membership vary wildly. In Tipperary eligibility for membership is usually automatic for persons living in the parish, though in some cases the committee are vested with the final say. A parish is likely to cover a number of square miles and is divided into townlands. Some townlands may be no more than a couple of hundred acres in extent and contain only one or two farms. Others can cover thousands of acres. For people living outside the parish there are likely to be special rules governing membership. In some cases a residents-only rule applies. In other cases there may be a waiting list even for residents. This may be necessary because the club has limited preserves or because game is scarce. I am not aware of any club in Tipperary which operates a waiting list for locals. The matter of outsiders is often complicated by the fact that people living well away from the parish have relations, possibly landowners, living in the parish. Ireland, like most countries and western Europe, has seen and continues to see a drift of people to urban areas. In our case to the fast growing conurbations of the eastern seaboard. It is very hard, if not impossible, for a club to refuse membership to, say, a farmer's son living in Dublin when the farmer has allowed the club the use of his lands.

Clubs approach these sorts of problems in different ways. In some cases the application for membership has to be properly proposed and seconded at an AGM and then put to a vote of members. The rules of our local club were drawn up by a crafty old Garda Sergeant who was secretary for many years. He was clearly a man who felt that it should not be too easy for an outsider to enjoy the fruits of the club's preserves. Essentially, if someone living outside the parish wanted to join the club they had to be voted in at an AGM. But there were two caveats. Three quarters of the membership had to be present at the meeting and they had to return a two thirds majority in favour of the application. Unsurprisingly, the club did not have many members domiciled elsewhere. I can only recall the very occasional meeting at which we had three quarters of the membership present. Nowadays that draconian rule has been modified and an outsider has a reasonable chance of joining the club.

The Splendid Variety of Rough Shooting

Away from the forest, a late November day's shooting may well start off with a visit to the river bank or a few ponds in search of mallard. It is unlikely to have seen much shooting during the week so there is a fair chance of a positive start to the day. After this the usual haunts will require attention. Rushy fields are well worth a visit as there should be plenty of snipe about in addition to the odd pheasant. If there is some rough cover at the edge of the rushes it may deliver up a woodcock or two. Ponds and drains should not be neglected and a detour from the chosen route could be rewarded with a few teal in the bag. As ever, weather conditions will have a big say in the proceedings. Should the Sunday stay dry there will probably be a second session after a long and leisurely lunch. Finally the day may be capped off with an evening flight of duck or pigeons. A wet day is likely to bring about an abrupt end to proceedings. There are few things less enjoyable than beating through heavy cover in persistent rain. Anyway pheasants quickly tire of wet conditions underfoot and are likely to go up to roost hours before dusk.

To borrow part of a phrase from Charles Dickens, the cock pheasant can bring out the best in men and the worst in men. A story of saints and sinners. As is all too often the case, the work of the saints goes unnoticed and uncommented upon. Yet countless sportsmen in the gun clubs in Ireland give willingly of their time in a range of conservation activities. However, it is upon the sinners that I intend to focus. Sinners, the world over, are invariably more interesting characters than saints.

The shooting man has yet to be born who will pass through life without committing some minor transgressions in the course of his adventures with dog and gun. But the real sinners are those who have honed their transgressions to a fine art. These customers can come from any age group, any background and any calling in life. My all-time favourite was a man who lived in these parts and who had a passion for pheasant shooting. Strangely, I do not think that he ever actually connected with a bird. This, though, did not appear to be a deterrent and his enthusiasm for the chase remained with him well into old age. In deference to him, he has now passed on to Paradise, we will refer to him simply as John. A perfectly normal, decent man until the dog pointed at his side of the ditch. After that it was all downhill. As the dog went in to flush the pheasant he would roar 'Watch out' to his companion at the other side of the ditch and simultaneously fire at the point from which he assumed the bird would exit the ditch. The pheasant and the shot charge would come out together, usually several feet apart. Quite clearly this somewhat unique brand of hunting did little for the mental wellbeing of his companion. With one exception I never heard of a man who went back for a second experience. The exception was one of the most placid and easy going men that I have ever met. He never seemed to be particularly concerned that he might return from a shooting trip minus a significant part of his anatomy. I asked him once how he managed to cope with these near suicidal missions. He told me that he saw no real problem. As soon as John began to shout he simply dived to the ground.

Transgressions

On one occasion in early November this sporting duo invited me to join them for a morning's shooting. Having heard so many stories of John's exploits it was with no small degree of trepidation that I agreed to accompany them. The expedition began, and for me ended, on a farm in which there were four adjoining beet fields each surrounded by tall blackthorn ditches. Ideal pheasant country. We had scarcely entered the first of these fields when Bruce pointed. Forgetting, in the intensity of the moment, John's hard earned reputation, I moved up behind the dog. A miserable half-grown cock that had yet to grow a tail fluttered into the air. It was immediately awarded a two-barrel salute from just over my shoulder which left my ears ringing for the next half hour. The baby cock, unmoved by the experience, landed in an ash tree in the ditch no more than twenty yards away. From its perch it looked down on us with a baleful eye, emitting the occasional chirp. It had not yet learned to crow.

John then proceeded to do what I thought was impossible. He reloaded, took careful aim and missed. At this juncture I suddenly remembered a long standing engagement and beat a hasty retreat.

Pheasants, it must be said, have a habit of leading men into sin. They begin to do so soon after the season has started — by seeking out forbidden places and taking up residence. To make matters worse they then go to great lengths to make their presence obvious by disporting themselves in fields next to the road and crowing extra loudly at dusk. The forbidden places may be club sanctuaries, farms which have been preserved by the owner and, not uncommonly, yards or haggards in the proximity of a farmhouse. In fairness sanctuaries are generally observed, though outsiders may occasionally make a sweep if they think that they can get away with it. It is the yards and haggards that give rise to more problems than any other places. As often as not a farmer will allow shooting over his lands. However, he or his wife are apt to become attached to pheasants that move in with them. They may even start

A snapshot at a woodcock breaking from cover.

to feed them. Sometimes these birds will be seen in the early morning perched on a cattle trough waiting for the next supply of food. When, as the season passes, birds become scattered and scarce, otherwise law abiding sportsmen may be tempted to partake of this forbidden fruit. The inevitable result is a mighty row.

Some devious gentlemen of my acquaintance will go to considerable lengths to shoot one of these birds. Why I have no idea. Having grown partly tame due to regular human presence they do not present anything approaching a sporting challenge. Yet they have a magnetic effect which will not be sated until they are safely in the bag. Years ago, when most people in the parish went to 11 o'clock Mass on a Sunday morning, there was, in the modern idiom, a recurring window of opportunity. Many a handsome cock met his maker whilst his erstwhile benefactor was engaged in a monologue with the same maker.

Other than in the case of the driven shoots there has been little attempt in Ireland to make the pheasant the subject of commercial shooting. The few attempts that have been made have, to my knowledge, been anything but successful. Realistically everything militates against such an operation. For rough shooting a relatively large area has to be preserved, stocked and keepered. Predator levels alone would cause serious difficulties, to say nothing of preventing incursions by locals who have traditionally shot the ground.

A good number of years ago a gentleman in another county decided to supplement his income by means of such an endeavour. He already brought in Italians to shoot pigeons in the summer and had permissions to extend his empire. This was at a time when the gun club movement was still in its infancy. Being a canny sort of a fellow and realising that many released birds would not survive long in the wild he hit upon an ingenious solution. Many of us, as children in rural Ireland, took great delight in putting farmyard hens to sleep by tucking their heads under a wing and then gently rocking them from side to side. When put back on the ground they would stay motionless for a considerable time. I am not sure whether they were actually asleep or simply traumatised by this unconventional treatment. These, incidentally, were real hens such as Rhode Island Reds and Light Sussex which, sadly, have now been replaced by some amorphous brand of broiler which has even lost the instinct to go broody.

OBLIGING PHEASANTS

Anyway, the gentleman in question reared a couple of hundred fine pheasants in his back yard. He had always been interested in rearing birds and was a dab hand with an incubator in an era in which the said machines were anything but reliable. Shooting parties, usually four in number, were booked in for Saturday mornings. An hour or so before their arrival this entrepreneur-extraordinary would put a half dozen of

Discussing the events of the afternoon: the end of a woodcock shoot.

his cock pheasants into a sack and set off on a tour of his preserves. At appropriate locations such as a clump of furze or brambles he would take a cock from the sack, put it to sleep in the prescribed manner and stuff it under the cover. There the unfortunate bird would remain until the later arrival of the shooting party.

In order to provide value for money the morning's sport consisted of rabbits as well as pheasants. These positively abound in most places having made an almost complete recovery from myxomatosis which had been brought into Ireland in the mid-1950s. No one seems to shoot them anymore, other than in the name of crop protection. In my childhood they were eaten regularly, but once myxomatosis came they were quickly deleted from the menu.

Our hero always ensured that the pheasants were sufficiently well spread to allow rabbit shooting without bringing the birds back to full consciousness. Unaware of how the pheasants had reached their 'hiding' places the shooting guests were in positive awe of the man. Approaching one of the appointed drop points he would gesture for them to be quiet and whisper that this was a likely place for a bird. On cue the dog would point and in the fullness of time the cock would emerge only to fall in a positive hail of lead. His fieldcraft was nothing less than superb. If he said there would probably be a bird, then a bird there would be. Almost invariably the six cocks that left his yard in the early morning would make a return in a rather different state some hours later. It was rumoured, though I cannot confirm it, that some of the stupefied cocks simply staggered out of the cover in response to much kicking of the bushes. It was further rumoured that his guests did not seem to see much wrong with this and shot them anyway.

I never heard what finally happened to this rather unusual shoot. It seemed, in financial terms, very much like a winner. I suspect that with the rise and expansion of the gun club movement it was eventually consigned to its unique pigeon hole in history.

Full Board and Shooting

A very different project had but a brief existence. Not too far from here is a very scenic area in which, pre-EEC, farmers had to work hard and long to make a decent living. A group of them decided to set up a rough shoot for European visitors. The idea was to release pheasants on their lands and, in addition to the shooting, develop bed and breakfast facilities. Initially everything went smoothly but then, after a couple of years, the visitors ceased to make bookings. Having got to know the area the ex-clients booked into a hotel in a nearby town and proceeded to shoot the lands for free. Nowadays there is a flourishing gun club in the area and the bed and breakfasts rely in the main on a summer trade.

Partridge shooting also begins on 1st November. Until about a decade ago this meant a two-week season for the native grey partridge. Despite its very greatly reduced numbers the shooting fraternity was most anxious to retain this short open season.

There were two extremely good reasons for this. A number of gun clubs, with pride of place going to those in County Wexford, were making sterling efforts to revive the fortunes of the species by means of ongoing breeding and release programmes. They were not shooting the birds, indeed the vast majority of sportsmen were granting them safe passage. The one stimulus that these clubs had needed was an expectation that at some time in the future they would reap the rewards of their endeavours by shooting partridges once again. When officialdom, as ever backed by those who see themselves as the only true conservationists, took away the season there was an immediate corollary. Clubs simply stopped releasing partridges. Whatever hope there was for a revival of the species' fortunes in Ireland, it was swept away by armchair conservationists.

The second reason why the shooting fraternity was anxious to retain a nominal season was that it knew only too well of the extraordinary difficulty involved in getting a bird restored to the shooting list once it had been removed. In an earlier chapter I outlined the story of duplicity surrounding the removal of wild geese from the Open Seasons Order.

Nowadays, therefore, partridge shooting in Ireland refers to red-legs. This is a species native to southern Europe. It is found, in particular, in Spain, Portugal and parts of France and Italy. It is not native to Ireland and Britain. In the late 1970s the National Association of Regional Game Councils, being conscious of the grey partridge's problems and the poor returns then being obtained from pheasant releases, decided to investigate the possibility of introducing new game birds. The list of possible candidates for introduction was clearly limited. In Britain the only alien game bird other than the pheasant to successfully survive a transplant was the red-leg. It appeared logical therefore, to look at this species as a potential candidate for introduction.

RELEASING THE RED-LEGS

Over three hundred years ago attempts were made to establish the red-leg in Britain. The first of these attempts appears to date back to around 1673. As with most introductions of exotic species, progress was slow and a century was to elapse before the red-leg really began to take root. Large scale releases in Sussex between the years 1770 and 1790 would seem to have laid the foundation of the present wild population. Then, as is the case with the pheasant, this wild population was augmented annually by very large scale poult releases. I can find very little information about attempts to introduce the red-leg to Ireland.

In his book *The Naturalised Animals of the British Isles*, Christopher Lever records that a Mr Gilda attempted to introduce red-legs into County Galway before 1844. he also records that a single bird was shot near Clonmel, County Tipperary on 4th February 1849. Where this bird came from is a matter of conjecture. I can only presume that many other attempted introductions were both unsuccessful and unrecorded.

The investigation into the possibility of introducing the red-leg under the auspices of the National Association of Regional Game Councils began in 1979 and ran for three years. The project sought to assess the likelihood of a successful introduction, to establish management techniques for rearing and releasing that would be suited to the Irish conditions and to encourage gun clubs to participate in the proceedings. A subsidiary objective of the investigation was to prepare guidelines for possible future introduction attempts as this is an area of game bird management for which the literature is very sparse.

The first step was to carry out a desk-top study of climatic conditions in the red-leg's native range, in Britain and in Ireland. Rainfall and temperature in particular were looked at as they could be critical factors in determining the success or failure of an attempted introduction. Over its native range the red-leg is found in areas with an annual rainfall of between 250mm and 890mm per year. Practically all of eastern Britain, the red-leg's main stronghold, receives less than 800mm per year and many areas receive less than 600mm. In contrast, most parts of eastern Ireland receive between 750mm and 1000mm, mainly near the upper end of the range. As rainfall is likely to be especially critical during the breeding season on account of its direct effect on chicks and on the all-important supply of insect life, comparative figures were obtained for specific points in eastern Britain and eastern Ireland. Rainfall levels for two locations in each country will illustrate the situation.

Rainfall (mm)	Annual	April	May	June	July
Clogherhead (Co. Louth)	765	49	55	55	68
Dublin	764	45	60	58	70
Clacton	555	35	40	41	47
Skegness	583	38	44	44	57

As can be seen there is quite a substantial difference between the driest parts of England and Ireland. This difference might prove to be very significant because of a behavioural feature of red-leg chicks. Whereas the young of grey partridges forage close to their mother and quickly return to the cover she provides during periods of heavy rain, those of red-legs forage widely and are thus more likely to get a soaking. The resultant chilling and possible infection could have a major impact on brood survival. It is a recognised fact in Britain that red-legs perform badly in breeding terms

Coming home from the hill after a good morning's rough shooting.

Taking a crossing snipe.

during wet summers. Nevertheless, following its introduction into Britain, the red-leg did adapt to some degree to slightly wetter weather conditions as evidenced by its spread to the west and north.

Temperature fluctuations appear not to militate against successful introductions. Nowhere over the red-leg's native range does the mean temperature for the month of January fall below -1°C. In the case of Britain, the mean minimum does not fall beneath 0.6°C, and in the case of Ireland the mean minimum for January lies between 3.8°C and 6.2°C.

Consideration was also given to the relative significance of predation in Ireland and Britain. As we have already seen, predator control over large areas of Ireland is, in the absence of professional keepering, at best sporadic. For birds that roost on the ground there are serious implications, especially in the case of released ones that are not as worldly-wise as their truly wild cousins. Quite clearly, intensive and ongoing predator control in the release areas would have to be an imperative in any introduction attempt.

Following this initial assessment the next step was the acquisition of breeding stock. A pure strain of red-leg was obtained from a game farm in Worcestershire. This was vital because red-legs have been crossed with several related species, in particular rock partridges. The resulting hybrids are popular with game farmers because they are docile and lay large numbers of eggs. They would, however, have been totally unsuited to the Irish project because it appears their ability to breed successfully in the wild is extremely limited. Effectively, the hybrids are only of value in the put-and-take context. A year later the breeding flock was augmented by a further importation of pure strain birds, this time from a game farm in County Down in Northern Ireland.

During the first year of the project only pen mating was used. In the second and third years both pen and flock mating were employed. No significant difference was found between the two systems either in terms of the numbers of eggs produced or fertility. Flock mating would seem to be the most appropriate in the gun club context because of the much lower costs involved. Custom hatching was arranged at a nearby game

124

farm. At this farm pheasant eggs were set in the incubator every Thursday. As red-leg eggs take a day less to hatch they were taken to the game farm every Thursday evening so that they could be rested overnight before being put in the incubator the following morning.

Once the young poults were old enough to be taken off the lamp they were transferred to a movable pen or grass. The use of this pen was found to minimize disease problems. With a single exception the poults provided no management problems. The exception was foot picking which could break out at any time once the birds were beyond two weeks of age. If not acted upon as a matter of urgency the results could be extremely serious. The problem was solved by lightly de-beaking the chicks around two weeks of age.

In the first year of the project specially constructed temporary release pens were employed. This was the recommended method for partridge release. 'Coveys' of between seven and fifteen poults, minimum age 8½ weeks, were put in the pen. As far as possible the pen was sited in a sanctuary area adjacent to mixed tillage such as barley and potatoes. After a few days of acclimatisation the pen was opened in the very early morning and the poults simply walked out. A hopper outside the pen, identical to one with which the birds were familiar, coupled with the call bird effect of the next covey which had been immediately put into the pen helped to keep the new releases in the immediate vicinity, at least for a few days.

LESSONS LEARNT IN RELEASING RED-LEGS

After the first year the temporary release pen was abandoned because it appeared ill-suited to the requirements of a typical gun club. Maybe there are more stray dogs in Tipperary than elsewhere but they soon became an intolerable problem. On several occasions we found a dog in the pen in the early morning and the surviving poults scattered to the four winds. Another problem was that pheasants quickly found the hopper outside the pen and would be in attendance from dawn to dusk. The newly-released poults had little chance of competing with adult pheasants. In consequence, all future releases were carried out using a conventional pheasant release pen. They were released in the company of pheasant poults. It was found that nine week old red-leg poults could hold their own with six-week-old pheasants. The two species fed together in the pen without any signs of aggression and subsequently released themselves in the usual manner. Since quite a lot of gun clubs have a release pen this would seem to be the most convenient release procedure.

The fate of the released birds was studied using a number of methods. Chief amongst these were transect counts, carried out each morning approximately one hour after dawn, monthly flush counts using a pointer, regular contacts with farmers on whose lands the birds had been released and appeals for information concerning sightings in the local press. It was found that, despite best efforts being made to retain birds, the great major majority of red-legs vacated the immediate release area within days of being released. By October of each year only a small percentage were to be found within one thousand metres of the release pen. The figures for those remaining in that month were 30.4%, 22.6% and 23.3% respectively. At the same time reports would begin to come in of sightings, often at quite considerable distances from the point of release. Sightings were reported at points varying between 1 and 19.3 kilometres from release. The mean dispersal distance during the years of the project was 4 kilometres. This level of dispersal did not auger well for gun clubs operating on a strictly limited budget. There would be a little point in spending quite a lot of money if the outcome was to supply a neighbouring club with some extra shooting.

The coveys that remained within the area were kept under observation until break up

the following spring. The precise points at which they were sighted were plotted on aerial survey maps. This enabled us to work out habitat preferences and also get an idea of the area of each covey's home range. The mean area of the home ranges of red-legs was 44 hectares.

The single most important aspect of the study was to ascertain the level, if any, of breeding success in the wild. From mid-March sightings were predominantly of paired birds and over the three-year period twenty one pairs were located. The territories taken up by these pairs were mapped in the same manner as that employed for the winter home ranges. The mean territory area was 1.35 hectares. Breeding success, as evidenced by brood sightings, was recorded for eight of the twenty-one. The hens of two further pairs which had nested in roadside vegetation were killed by cars.

A third hen deserted her nest as a result of grass cutting operations. The sighting of broods was the good news. The bad news was that only three of them were seen after the very young chick stage. Of these three the oldest was a brood of eight 3-week-olds which were observed on the 5th, 6th and 8th August 1981. The mean brood size was 8.1, with a range of 5–11. In relation to rainfall it is pertinent to note that five of the eight broods were seen in July 1982, the only July in the study period in which rainfall was negligible.

Outside the main project centre in Tipperary a number of clubs were simultaneously releasing poults supplied by the project. They too attempted to ascertain the level of breeding success in the wild. Altogether they located thirteen broods, in almost all cases of very young chicks. The oldest was a brood of eight 2-week-olds seen in Termonfeckin, County Louth on 6th July 1981. As was the case in Tipperary the majority of brood sightings took place during the dry July of 1982.

What conclusions can be drawn from the project? It is, I believe, reasonable to propose that a viable wild population could be established in the driest part of Ireland: i.e. counties Louth, Dublin and parts of Meath. Rainfall levels in this region are just within the red-leg's natural range of tolerance. At the project centre in Tipperary mean annual rainfall is 961mm, a little on the high side. The fact, though, that released birds survived the winter and produced broods the following year is very positive.

If an introduction is to be successful a very large number of birds will have to be released, preferably over a good number of years. Herein lies a major difficulty. Few clubs or individuals are likely to be able to fund a release of sufficient magnitude. A glimmer of hope may come from another direction. In recent years the red-leg has gained popularity as a put-and-take species. It may possibly happen that these continuous releases will result in a steady flow of birds into the wild. These birds just might become the founders of a genuinely wild population.

Other than in the case of the red-leg, little has been done in the way of bringing alien game birds to Ireland in the modern era. From former times a few records exist of introductions of two species, the bobwhite quail and the black grouse. A third species the capercaillie, was also brought to Ireland but this was really an attempt at re-introduction.

The bobwhite quail is native to the south-eastern United States and is a great favourite with American sportsmen. Many attempts to naturalise the species in England were made in the nineteenth and twentieth centuries. In most cases the birds disappeared after a couple of years though in at least one case a wild population was known to survive

LEFT
Gathering up the pheasants at the edge of a wood.

BELOW
The end of a satisfactory duck flight.

for ten years after the release. Most recently bobwhites have been released with some degree of success in Suffolk and the Scilly Isles. R.S.R. Fitter records that the very first liberation of bobwhites in these islands took place in Ireland. A General Gabbit released a large number prior to 1813 but there is no indication as to where this took place. In any event they all disappeared within two years.

Hunting a rough corner for a pheasant or woodcock.

When the red-leg project was over in Tipperary a consignment of bobwhites was obtained. Some of the pens were modified and flock mating was employed for two years. This was extremely successful and vast numbers of eggs were obtained. Literally heaps of eggs could be found in clusters of nettles within the pen. Custom hatching was again arranged. Fertility was excellent and the tiny chicks were surprisingly resilient. No problems were encountered in rearing them to release age. At this juncture the good news comes to an abrupt end. A number of clubs in Tipperary and beyond released poults, in some instances in very large numbers. One club released nearly five hundred in one go. Without exception the outcome was the same. The quail stayed around for a few days and then, despite the provision of more than adequate food, simply disappeared. None were ever seen again. It has been suggested that, even if they had survived the winter, Irish springs are too wet and too cold for them.

The black grouse was widespread in Britain until the beginning of the nineteenth century, but there is no record of its presence on this side of the Irish Sea. It has always been a bird close to the hearts of sportsmen and many attempts were made to establish it in Ireland during the nineteenth century. Most of these involved birds caught up in Scotland. In a few cases the grouse were sourced in Scandanavia. All the attempted introductions ended in failure. Poachers were commonly blamed for these failures though it is much more likely that Mother Nature was responsible. I understand that black grouse were brought into Northern Ireland in the 1980s but I do not know whether any were actually liberated there.

There has been much debate as to whether the capercaillie was ever native to Ireland. The general consensus is that it was, but that it had become extinct before the beginning of the nineteenth century. This was probably as a result of deforestation. A record exists of what were probably capercaillies in Tipperary in the late 1750s. There are two recorded attempts to re-establish the capercaillie in Ireland. Both of these took place in the nineteenth century and both were unsuccessful.

The Brief Curlew Season

One other game bird season opens on 1st November. This is for the curlew. The season is confined to the month of November and in both opening date and duration it defies all logic. Curlews are common and widespread in Ireland and shooting poses no threat whatsoever to the population. Breeding birds are numbered in tens of thousands and are distributed across many counties. As early as August migrants begin to arrive, mainly from Britain and Scandanavia. By mid-winter there are probably between 100,000 and 200,000 in the country, most likely towards the upper limit. Some curlews remain on the coast whilst others come inland where they tend to favour pasture fields. When low-lying land floods the curlew packs are soon in evidence and, at dusk, are usually on the move before the duck. There is absolutely no reason why the season should be any different from that of other wading birds such as golden plover and snipe. That this is not the case is simply a matter of eco-politics (if such a word exists). The twitching fraternity have always had a soft spot for the curlew probably on account of its mournful call. It has been on and off the shooting list a number of times. Its present 'on' position is a sop to the shooting fraternity as a result of the removal of the white-fronted goose from the shooting list in the mid-1980s. When, at that time, the curlew shooting was restored, the predictable high-pitched clamour of protest arose. Indeed, if memory serves me correctly, a paper quickly appeared which suggested that the population was in trouble and needed to be protected.

I do not think that many curlews are shot, at least inland. On the coast I know of only a few individuals who enjoy flighting them over the mudflats at dawn. But that is their thing and good luck to them. I probably shoot no more than two or three in a season even though they are widespread in Tipperary from autumn onwards. If I were to be very honest, I would have to admit that most years I shoot one or two accidentally. Early in the evening there is no mistaking curlews as they swish up and down over the water. Even the super myopic are aware of their unique call. But in the gathering gloom towards the end of evening flight, single birds can sweep in across a flood very much in the manner of mallard. There are also times when curlews come in mixed flocks with duck. I can recall two occasions on which wigeon have whistled overhead and, on downing one, the dog has come back with a curlew.

December:
the Month of the Woodcock

ABOVE
The easy option!
Walking the edge of the
forest whilst the rest of
the troops do the hard
yards inside in search of
woodcock.

Left
A brace of woodcock,
showing the beautiful
feather markings which
enable the birds to
merge completely with
the forest floor.

Of the shooting months, December is my undoubted favourite. All the migrants are now in and there is a wonderful choice of quarry. Cock pheasants, admittedly, are getting a little thin on the ground, something that does not worry me unduly. There are still enough of them around to meet the requirements of those who seek them. Then there is the weather. Anything is possible in December. One day the ground is hard and the air crisp after a night of heavy frost. Another day yet more Atlantic squalls sweep in across the country leaving exciting-looking splashes in their wake. Of recent years wet and windy weather seems to be getting more common while frosts are becoming increasingly rare phenomena. Last winter I can recall no more than a handful of frosty mornings. As for snow, we are lucky if we see it in the lowlands more than once or twice a year. It must be twenty years or more since we had any serious and prolonged snow in this corner of Tipperary.

Above all else December is the month of the woodcock. Whilst we meet them with increasing frequency as November passes, it is not until December that serious woodcock shooting begins for us. If I had to list the various game birds in order of importance, to me the woodcock

131

would come in at number two. Only the red grouse, king of the wild high moorlands, ranks above it. On that same list snipe, the bread and butter of my shooting, would occupy third place. Two of these three do not enter mankind's civilized domain with anything like the frequency that other game birds do. It takes weather of an especially ferocious nature to drive grouse away from the heather. In my lifetime I have only seen grouse on grassy fields on a couple of occasions. By grassy fields, incidentally, I mean real green grass, as opposed to the wiry, yellow stuff that mixes with and fringes the heather. Woodcock generally restrict their visits to the haunts of humans to night time sorties, mainly to wet and boggy places.

Both in appearance and behaviour the woodcock is a bird apart. The long bill and widespread toes betray its wading nature, but a wader who only reveals the fact at dusk. Its plumage is a marvel of contrasting rufus, browns and blacks. Perfect camouflage for life on the bracken-strewn floor of its woodland home. The feathers of the wings and back vary from a very bright rufus to an almost greyish shade of brown. The big black eyes are quite extraordinary in their position. High up and to the sides of the head they effectively provide 360° vision. Because of this a predator will find it very hard to creep up on a feeding woodcock.

From time to time a short billed woodcock appears in the bag. The length of its bill in relation to that of a normal bird is reminiscent of the difference between the bills of jack and common snipe. There has been much debate concerning the short billed form. Is it a sporadic mutation or part of a process of evolution equipping it to feed at a different level in the soil to its normal cousins? My personal view is that it is no more than a spasmodic mutation. If the possession of a shorter bill were truly advantageous, one would expect it to be appearing more and more often. Quite frankly I cannot remember when I last shot a short billed bird. It was certainly a few years ago. The first time that I shot one was on a viciously cold morning in the early 1980s. An isolated stretch of furze on a hillside near here, which is usually good for a woodcock or two, produced seven or eight on that particular morning. I shot two and a companion shot a third, but it was not until we were emptying the bag several hours later that I noticed the unusual one. That winter was one of the coldest that I can remember. The only colder one in my lifetime was some twenty years earlier. During that particular winter the daytime temperature remained beneath 0°C for weeks on end. It had a devastating effect on bird life. Wood pigeons in particular died of starvation because they could not break through the frozen soil to feed. One morning I went out with a bucket of water to take the frost off the car's windscreen. As the water splashed everywhere a woodcock walked slowly out from under the car and took off on the most leisurely of flights.

Woodcock display a certain spirit of the wild in their behaviour. In March and April the roding flight of the males is something I find

LEFT
Good woodcock country. When flushed, woodcock will usually attempt an escape along a forestry thinning line.

BELOW
Replanted ground next to mature forestry can hold surprising numbers of woodcock at times.

fascinating and could watch for hours. In the early dusk they fly circuit after circuit over their woodland homes. This is not the fast, jinking flight of a woodcock flushed from cover. Rather it is slow and purposeful, a little owl-like if anything. Bird books record two very different calls during a roding flight. One is a frog-like croak, the other a high pitched whistling sound. Maybe Tipperary woodcock are men of few words. More often than not the ones that I see fly in silence. Occasionally I have heard one utter the croaking noise but I have never heard anything remotely like a whistle. On any one evening the length of the circuit seems to remain almost constant. I have sometimes timed a circuit and could then predict to within a few seconds when the bird would reappear. Roding also takes place in the half light of dawn but, I must confess, I have never risen to witness it.

It was previously thought that roding flights were territorial in nature. Territorial in the sense that a cock bird defends a given area of land in which he and his beloved rear a brood or two. Research has shown however that the cock is not devoted to a single partner. By flying around his domain he is advertising himself to any lady woodcock in the area. Should his large and beady eyes fall upon one of these ladies he will descend and attempt to mate.

In a very different way snipe also advertise their presence as their sex hormone levels rocket in the spring. Males produce a strange, almost unearthly sound as they dive from a height at an acute angle. This humming sound is caused by the vibration of tail feathers as the air rushes through them in the course of the dive. On rare occasions I have seen snipe performing in this manner in the early part of the shooting season.

A face mask is a handy accessory for duck shooting once daylight has come.

The woodcock's evening flight to its feeding grounds is much faster and more direct than the roding flight. In truly ancestral habitat woodcock may not fly at all at dusk. Places such as oak woodlands provide a sufficiency of earthworms to meet their needs as well as draught-free nooks in which to lie up during the daylight hours. But the spread of coniferous woodland has undoubtedly resulted in more dusk flighting. These new forests provide them with a variety of roosting sites but the impoverished soils of the floor are all but devoid of worms and the other invertebrates they need. In consequence the woodcock must move out under the security of darkness to obtain its supper.

In the late afternoon blackbirds in woodland engage in noisy chatter as they go to roost. Not long afterwards, but before it is dark enough for duck to move, the woodcock head out to their feeding grounds. An old mountain man of my acquaintance once told me that he reckoned that the reason why woodcock leave the forest at dusk is because they cannot stand any more of the noise that the blackbirds make.

In my experience woodcock do not travel far from the forest to feed. The first marshy field that they come to is frequently used. Sometimes they will drop to feed literally at the forest's edge. I have seen them come out, fifty or sixty feet up in the air, and swing around to land just next to the sheep netting that often guards plantations. On a windy night in winter woodcock come at knots and are gone almost as soon as they are seen. They follow fairly regular and traditional flight paths and can be as regular as clockwork. These flight paths follow routes devoid of aerial obstructions such as forest rides, thinning lines and even forest roads.

WOODCOCK BEHAVIOUR

A well-known feature of woodcock behaviour is the female's habit of carrying her young in flight between her legs. I have never been witness to this but would dearly love to see it. Whilst I have found the woodcock's nest with its chestnut blotched eggs I have only once seen the young. One of my sons was walking a springer on an April afternoon when it went off only to return with a well-fledged, two-thirds size woodcock. Minutes later it was back again with a second one of equal size. These two young birds were extremely lucky that the dog in question was by far the most soft-mouthed one that we possessed at the time. For birds of a wild forest they were surprisingly tame. The main problem in the days that followed was to find enough earthworms to keep them happy. They had insatiable appetites: every time that we went near them they would open their long bills in the expectation that yet another juicy worm would be dropped in. Finally I got fed up with feeding them and gave them to a friend, a great lover of woodcock and a great woodcock shot. He brought them to maturity and then freed them in a wood near his house. I have often wondered whether, having become so used to being fed, they survived for long.

Published figures for the resident woodcock population lie in the range 4,000–5,000 pairs, much too low an estimate in my opinion. With the spread of forestry of recent years a vast amount of extra breeding sites has become available. By mid-winter the number of woodcock in the country is enormous. One can only hazard a guess but it must be several hundred thousand. Many of the migrant population originate in Britain, but substantial numbers also come from Scandanavia and the Baltic States. The rate of immigration increases dramatically as November proceeds and continues in December. As is the case with teal, further immigration may occur in late winter if the European mainland is subjected to harsh weather.

Over thirty years ago the Cork Federation of Gun Clubs set out to investigate the relative proportions of native and migrant woodcock. Cork is a county renowned for the species, especially in parts of the southwest. Over a five year period, commencing in 1968, they organised flush counts in many areas of the county. These counts were conducted during the last week of March and the last week of November in each of the years. As woodcock are early breeders (it is not unusual to find completed clutches at the end of March) the birds counted in that month were assumed to be residents. Those counted in November were both resident and migratory. The November counts were slightly over ten times greater than the March ones, suggesting that resident woodcock represent some 9% of the mid-winter population. As there is further immigration well into December it would appear that the resident population represents only a tiny fraction of the winter one.

I always make a point of checking the age group to which the woodcock that I shoot belong. The relative proportion of young to adults gives a good indication of the level of breeding success. The method for doing this, which was devised in Denmark, is relatively simple and I commend it to all sportsmen. It relies upon certain features of the plumage but, for simplicity, one is all-important. There is a significant difference between the state of the trailing edges of the primary (outer) wing feathers of adult and young birds. If the wing is held up to the light and the feathers spread out, one of two observations will normally be made. In adults the trailing edges of the feathers will be smooth and unbroken whereas in the year's young they will show varying degrees of being worn and tattered. The difference is due to the age of the feathers. The young have been flying on the same ones since they first took to the air in April or May. As they lift from cover and flit through the trees there is inevitable abrasion which wears away the trailing edges. In contrast, adult birds moult after the breeding season, usually between mid-July and September and so fly on much newer feathers for much of the shooting season. These typically show little or no wear and tear. In the vast majority of cases I find little difficulty in assigning a woodcock to its correct age group.

Older Birds, Longer Journeys

The proportion of young birds is always much lower in Ireland than in Britain. This has been explained by the length of the migratory journeys that they must undertake. Scandanavian and Baltic birds must first cross the North Sea. Young birds, it would seem, are then less willing to make a second hop across the Irish Sea. I suppose in consideration of their relative strengths this makes sense.

Snipe can also be aged by reference to the primary wing feathers though I find that the differences are not nearly as clear cut as they are in the case of woodcock. I assume that this is because snipe, living in more open conditions, subject their flight feathers to much less abrasion when they take to the air. With any batch of snipe wings which I attempt to age there are always a few that are not clear cut.

Traditionally in Ireland woodcock were shot from 1st September until the last day of February. February was always considered to be a great month as woodcock numbers were higher than at any other time of year. Then, over the years, the season was gradually whittled down. The opening day was moved back to 1st October and then 1st November. At the other end the closing date was brought forward to 31st January. I have little argument with this later change. Since most of our woodcock are migratory it makes good sense to give them a reasonable period of rest and undisturbed feeding before they set out on those long flights to their breeding grounds. However, at the other end there was no need whatsoever to abbreviate

Waiting for the start of the next assault on a woodcock stronghold.

the season. Woodcock hatch early and by September are quite fit to be hunted. If snipe, as is undoubtedly the case, are fair game in September, then so too are woodcock. Shooting men, or rather a small minority of them, must take some responsibility for the move from October to November. It occurred in part because of claims that woodcock shooting in woodland and scrub was leading to a premature opening of the pheasant season. Maybe the odd cock pheasant was shot but, as far as I know, it was anything but a common occurrence. It should not have been allowed as an excuse to deprive the great majority of decent sportsmen of a month's woodcock shooting.

As a result of the passage into law of the Wildlife Act in the mid-1970s another restriction on woodcock shooting was imposed. Shooting of the species was confined to the period beginning at sunrise and ending at sunset. Woodcock flighting at dusk, in my book one of the most exciting and demanding forms of game bird shooting, was thus outlawed. This provision of the Act was sneaked in surreptitiously without the majority of woodcock shooters being made aware of it. Officialdom, at the time, stated that the provision was necessary because woodcock were being 'slaughtered' as they left their woodland homes at dusk. Nothing could have been further from the truth but it made no difference. The matter was done and dusted. I can only repeat what I said at the time. That same officialdom should have been required to stand out at the forest's edge on a freezing winter's evening and see at first hand just how difficult it can be to shoot woodcock under such conditions.

Top class dogs are an absolute essential for woodcock shooting. Different people have different preferences; some friends of mine, for

example, will countenance nothing but setters for the task, but, to me, dogs in this instance means only one thing. Springers. And, specifically, springers with big hearts which will take on any cover. I have owned many springers, some a bit lethargic, some non-stop triers, some generally good but lacking that killer instinct that would propel them through a brick wall if there were a woodcock on the other side. They can display an incredible range of temperaments. Of them all one stood supreme, a handsome little bitch named Phoebe who was my pride and joy. I have never come across a dog with greater courage. Or, for that matter, greater intelligence. She came to me as a slightly shy two-year-old. Initially her role in life was that of a retriever of birds, something at which she excelled. It was when she was so engaged that I became aware that this was a dog apart.

Whatever the water conditions she never refused. If she did not return with the duck, a rare event, it was because the running tide or spate-fuelled river swept it away faster than she could swim. There were times when I thought that I would never see her again; a distant dot growing smaller and smaller as she made a valiant attempt to retrieve a bird being carried out to sea. On fast-running rivers she was apt to emerge with her prize many of hundreds of yards downstream. Once safely back on the bank she would put the duck down, give herself a good shake and return to me as if all this was the most natural thing in the world.

Above all else it was a really rough sea that set her apart from other dogs. On days when the hardiest of labradors stood back from the crashing waves, in she would go. Minutes later one would see a mallard or wigeon being propelled towards one, Phoebe's head totally obscured by the duck. Nor was cold a deterrent to her. One vicious late December morning I shot a teal just after dawn which fell well out in the Suir. It was

A new plantation alongside an existing one. Woodcock will lie out here on balmy days towards the end of the season.

138

one of those mornings when the sheer coldness of the air took the breath away. In no time at all Phoebe had the teal on the bank. Next, as usual, came the customary shake. I still cannot help but smile at the result. Her wet hair, fully erect with the cold, immediately froze. There in front of me was the nearest thing that you will ever see to a chocolate and white hedgehog.

Once Phoebe started accompanying me in pursuit of woodcock she showed herself to be a natural. Whether it was furze, brambles or hazels they were searched, and searched diligently. The great thing was that she seemed to know that she was expected to work close to me. There is nothing worse in woodcock shooting to my mind than half-mad springers crashing away a hundred yards ahead, driving all before them. There are many times when, in heavy cover, a woodcock leaves unseen. One is aware only of that special noise that results when fast beating wings come into contact with vegetation. If Phoebe was responsible for the flush one could be certain sure that, though unseen, the woodcock was in range.

Phoebe died young; she had not reached her sixth birthday. I will always blame myself for her premature end. She was the only dog that we ever possessed that was not confined to a pen. In her non-working life she doubled up as a family pet and spent her time sleeping on the sofa in the living room. Other than going out to respond to the call of nature she never ventured far from the house. Whenever I was home to watch the six o'clock news she would invariably hop up next to me. One lovely April evening she must have got fed up with the news as she slipped off the sofa and went outside. I thought nothing of her departure. Then, some ten minutes later, the door bell rang. A very pleasant young man clearly distraught, was there. He asked if the dog on the road belonged to us. Going out I found Phoebe thrown on the verge; frothy scarlet blood from her mouth and nose told the inevitable story. Why she had ventured onto the road I will never know. It had never happened before. Clearly, some minutes before our informant arrived on the scene, some sub-human creature had struck her and driven on, leaving her to die.

Some eighteen months earlier Phoebe had given birth to her one and only litter. She had thirteen pups. It had been our intention to breed from her once more so we kept only one of them, a dog. Orka, now six, has some of his mother's traits. He is a more than solid performer but, whether it is in water or in covers, he will never really match his mother.

A Perfect Day Woodcock Shooting

If I could design a day that would amount to perfection for me in terms of woodcock shooting it would be something like the following. First the place. A glen, with sides not too steep, running for several miles down a hillside. A stream, shrouded with heavy cover in places, bare banked in others, would run the length of the glen. In some stretches the stream would flow freely, in others it would hardly move, especially where the sallies overhang. In these latter places the edges of the stream, never experiencing the heat of the sun, would be soft and muddy. The bushes at each side of the glen would stretch back from the water's edge for some ten or eleven yards. In places, patches of furze would add to the width of the cover. Stretching back from the bushes the hillside would be swathed in a tight mass of bracken. Further out still there would be oldish heather, maybe a foot or two in height.

Second the weather. There would actually be two options. For preference the day would dawn cold and frosty. A typical December day of my childhood. It would have been frosty for two or three nights beforehand as well, with daytime temperatures hovering around 0°C. The minds of woodcock should have been concentrated by these conditions and caused them to seek the worm-rich mud at the edges of the stream. Snipe, too, would probably be present on account of the freezing conditions. They will add variety to the day. This is why I ordained that stretches of the stream should have bare banks. Snipe are not great lovers of heavy cover, even under the most extreme of conditions.

In an age of global warming my second weather scenario would be that of a balmy period which we are wont to get, most years, in late January or February. Then the woodcock would have moved back from the muddy ground and, if they have read my script, be sunning themselves in the pleasant warmth of the bracken or heather. This alternative weather scenario is second for no better reason than the purely emotive one that shooting at its best is a winter business. However, I will never allow myself to be accused of bias. I am just as happy to shoot woodcock in balmy weather as I am when the ground is crisp with frost.

Third, my companions. Three criteria will operate here. First of all they must own superb springers. I will define a superb springer in the words of a good friend and woodcock aficionado. He once said that his best springer hated woodcock. Sometimes the said hound and hater of woodcock would be fast enough to whip a few feathers from a departing tail. On other occasions he would dissolve into melancholy barking having failed to catch the object of his hate. A superb woodcock dog. Next, the said companions would be proficient woodcock shots. Woodcock and snipe shooting is a specialised art, a lot of it is snap shooting, and requires men of cool and relaxed temperament. Finally, and all-important, the companions must have a sense of occasion. This means that one of them must make the hard yards through the covers, urging the dogs on. And this no matter how heavy the cover is . The other companion will always insist that I walk on the side of the glen from which the woodcock usually emerge. I would, of course, not be upset if the odd bird went his way.

Now back to reality. Those lovely woodcock glens of the west and southwest of Ireland are anything but common in this part of Tipperary. Instead we must rely heavily on conifer plantations for most of our woodcock shooting. There are still spots with scrub cover and patches of furze but few of these extend to much more than a few acres. Other than these, the odd woodcock will be flushed from the heavier ditches in the course of pheasant shooting trips. Periods of hard weather can force woodcock down to farmland. On a really frosty December morning there is always a good chance of meeting them in cover along the banks of small rivers and streams. But, the instant the weather softens, they are off again to their woodland haunts.

Sitka spruce is by far the most common plantation tree. In purely economic terms it is well suited to Irish conditions. It grows quickly in our mild, moist climate and has a good tolerance of poor soils such as are found on mountain sides. There are few hills in Tipperary which have escaped the onward march of the sitka monoculture. For woodcock sitka is not an ideal species but it can deliver the goods at certain stages of the plantations development. In the early years woodcock will lie out in the heavy vegetation if the weather is mild and sunny. But the shooting is far from easy. There can be few worse places to walk than land that has been recently reafforested. As well as the old stumps of the previous plantation there are humps and hollows left by the timber-extracting machinery, new drainage channels and the ever-present scattering of rocks. Any woodcock shot is a woodcock hard-earned. But within a few years the young trees form a dense, impenetrable cover of absolutely no value to woodcock, or for any other bird for that matter. It is not until the first thinning, which I think comes around the fifteenth year of the plantation's life, that the forest begins to attract birds. The heaps of thinnings from the removed trees provide cover and there are now flight corridors available for entry and exit. If there are open places where the trees failed, bramble patches may develop. Equally, places that were too wet to plant develop a rushy covering and can deliver a bird or two. Successive thinnings in the plantation as it matures help to make it more attractive. More light can get in and this encourages growth of ground cover, especially ferns.

The ways of woodcock have always been something of a mystery. One can walk a big tract of forest and meet only the odd one. Then, in a relatively small area, the dogs can put half a dozen or more into the air. A week later that well-populated spot is quite likely to be totally devoid of them. In theory woodcock like to lie up in cosy places well sheltered from the wind and rain. They rarely stay in the forest for long if the weather turns wet and the spruce needles begin to drip unrelentingly. The real art of woodcock shooting is to find the cosy places.

In the early years of afforestation, lodgepole pine was planted on ground considered to be too poor for spruce. This, effectively, meant the higher ground, perhaps above one thousand feet, where the peat is shallow and rock erupts through it. Up here these trees rarely grow properly. A combination of nutrient deficiency and regular batterings from the wind have kept most of them small and stunted. Many died. The result, in our mountains, is some very attractive woodcock habitat. The lodgepole forests, if such they may be called, are extremely sparse and have a generous understorey of heather and bracken. Other than in very wet or very windy conditions they always hold a few birds. The great thing, from the shooting point of view, is that one can see one's neighbouring guns. Woodcock tend to fly low rather than high if there

Let proceedings commence. The line is about to enter the forest.

is plenty of space between the trees so the possible danger is all-too real. I find that a flushed woodcock usually only goes high if confronted by trees or tall vegetation at the point of flush.

Though it does not provide habitat of the same quality as lodgepole, larch is infinitely preferable to sitka spruce. Being deciduous, light can get in with the result that the ground cover is often quite reasonable. Around here, stands of larch were set on dry ground and as a result there is a good variety of plants on the forest floor. I have never shot a big bag of woodcock in a larch forest but there are usually sufficient to keep one alert.

The landlords of old were great men for their woodcock shooting. Without the forests of the present day to disperse the birds they were able to lure large numbers into relatively small areas by planting stands of hazel, alder and other species. These covers were fenced off from livestock and jealously guarded. There would be no more than a couple of shoots a year which might occupy several consecutive days, a full week in one case. Not surprisingly enormous bags were made. At one shoot in County Mayo in 1910 the bag for a week was 571.

Amongst the shrubs that were brought to Ireland to enhance the habitat for woodcock was the rhododendron. Not a good idea. Small clumps with moist ground under the foliage will hold woodcock but this plant is able to spread like wildfire. Great stretches of rhododendron cover up the ground giving dank and inhospitable surroundings with no means of entry or exit. As well, native species such as holly are quickly

On to the next block of forestry.

displaced and the regeneration of native oak woodland is made extremely difficult.

There is a scenic area in Tipperary which has been overrun by this alien. Once, and never again, I chanced a short cut back to the car through rhododendrons. It would have been easier to traverse a rain forest. Another shrub widely planted for the benefit of woodcock was the fuchsia. As the plants mature they bend over and provide moist tunnels ideal for both roosting and feeding. Brought from South America, the fuchsia never became a pest. The attractive magenta-coloured flowers can still be seen adorning roadside ditches in many of the more remote and mountainous parts of the country.

Depending upon circumstances woodcock can provide anything from the most testing of snap shots to relatively straightforward going away and crossing shots. A lot depends upon the terrain. Most of our sport takes place in forest or heavy scrub and the real problem is to get the gun onto the bird before it is lost from sight. Often as not it has already disappeared before the shot has left the barrel. But if the eye/hand co-ordination is reasonable, the dog will appear with the bird. If he does not it is well worthwhile to look closely at the lower branches as woodcock often fall into them.

Some people drive woodcock. Personally I have no problem with a few friends organising an impromptu drive in the course of a day's shooting. However, I strongly disapprove of large scale driving such as takes place on some of the commercial shoots. I see little sport in surrounding a cover and then putting in two or three beaters and their dogs. Most of the time it is little more than a slaughter and unworthy of one of the most elusive and sporting of birds. The problem is that the clients of commercial shoots want big bags and have neither the inclination nor the stamina to shoot woodcock properly, by slogging the hard miles for a possible reward of no more than a couple of birds.

The Ultimate Sporting Challenge

A right and left at woodcock is traditionally regarded as the pinnacle of the sport. That it is a relatively uncommon occurrence is more due to the fact that most encounters are with single birds than to the actual difficulty of shooting them. In forest shooting there is rarely the time to discharge a second barrel should a pair flush unless one is lucky enough to be in a broad clearing or ride. On those balmy days when the woodcock are lying out in the heather the right and left is not that difficult a challenge. I would regard a pair of snipe as being more difficult.

My first right and left at woodcock turned out to be something rather different. It was in those days before we were banned from shooting woodcock at dusk. Not far behind a particular farmyard there were two small lakes, maybe covering in total a couple of acres, which we called the farm lakes. They were, and indeed still are, great places to flight teal once winter arrives. For some reason mallard visit regularly during September but rarely after that. The lakes are surrounded by a spruce forest. Running down the middle of the plantation is a broad ride cleared to accommodate an electricity line. Waiting for teal we would occasionally see a woodcock passing down this ride and across the lakes. Then, as the years went by and the plantation matured, the evening woodcock traffic increased and we started to flight them before the teal came in. One evening I was there alone and had just settled into position when I spotted a woodcock coming with a second one only yards behind it. The two birds duly fell and I was delighted with my 'right and left'. Until, that is, the dog came back with my second bird. A sparrowhawk. Years later, in very different circumstances I gave a repeat performance of this unusual act. A cousin of mine owned a particularly fine farm for shooting which adjoined the Suir. He recently sold it and as a result I have lost one of my favourite shooting haunts. Anyway, the fields at the very back of the farm used to flood every winter and attract sizeable numbers of wigeon. To get to these fields for evening flight one followed an overgrown passage which fell steeply away behind the house. At intervals along this passage were gaps that gave access to the water meadows. Not long before evening flight I had emerged from one of these gaps when a woodcock suddenly appeared. As I shot it a second one appeared which I also shot.

Once again my second 'woodcock' turned out to be a sparrowhawk.

TYPICAL DECEMBER SUNDAY ROUGH SHOOT

A typical December Sunday will start for us, as indeed it did in November, with a quick check on the mallard and teal situation on the river. After that, according to preference, it will be a case of pheasant or snipe. A good cock may have been spotted during the week or a tip-off may require investigation. The afternoon will be devoted to woodcock and, as the evenings are short at this time of year, this means an early lunch.

Usually about half a dozen of us meet up for the afternoon session. This sort of number is necessary in order to ensure adequate cover of each block of trees. These blocks tend to be on the large side, some extending to several hundred acres. If one or two more guns are available so much the better, but not too many more for safety's sake. The whistle of an ounce plus of number seven shot in close proximity to one's person is not one of the more enjoyable sounds of the shooting field. We probably only shoot each of our best places a couple of times in a season, once in December and once in January.

My favourite place for this Sunday afternoon excursion is an afforested hillside which provides shooting for several miles of tough walking. We start by driving up a forestry road to a height of some five hundred feet. Then it is about half a mile to the point at which, hopefully, action will commence. A broad tract twists and turns up the hill from where we leave the cars until it runs into open heather. In places the gradient is steep and the path deeply rutted by winter floods. In other places it is almost ridiculously smooth and flat. To the right going up, the ground falls several hundred feet to a roaring, splashing and tumbling river. For most of the way on this side the trees are nearly mature sitka, by now well spaced following a number of thinnings. Towards the top are lodgepole pines, increasingly scattered with altitude. As they become more spread out the understorey of heather becomes increasingly dense. On the left side of the track, sitka gives way to lodgepole pines lower down, probably the single biggest block of pine in our territory. As a general rule this is by far the best side for woodcock.

We shoot the right hand side first as we go up. This leaves the best wine until last. Young and/or very fit men go down as far as the river at the forest's edge. A line is then formed and men of mature years vie for the privilege of walking the actual track. On a bad day as few as two or three woodcock may rise to test the reflexes of the advancing line. Eventually the line will emerge onto open mountain. Near the top, where the trees thin out, the dogs may, on a good day, persuade up to a dozen birds to forsake the security of the heather. But we will usually be content if we have a couple in the bag at this stage. On most occasions there is only one gun on the track though more may emerge from the forest as stamina levels plummet. A good case can be made for two guns on the track, one eighty yards or so ahead of the line and a second the same distance behind. Woodcock, more often than not, tend to fly downhill when flushed. Even those that escape in front are likely to swing high and curl back. Many a time I have seen the lone gun on the track stand and watch in despair as a bird crossed too far

Long-billed and short-billed woodcock – all shot in the same area of county Waterford.

in front or too far behind. When the gun on the track is ahead of the line it is imperative that the gun nearest to him keeps that fact in sharp focus. There is always a better than evens chance that a woodcock will make for the open space flying no more than two or three feet above the ground.

Out on the heather there is time for a short rest before the really serious business of the afternoon commences. The dying band of nicotine addicts amongst us, who had insufficient lung capacity to pull on the evil weed on the way up, can snatch a quick pull before we set off. Be in no doubt the activity of the last hour or so was strenuous in the extreme. The line of guns was moving steadily upwards whilst walking on a lateral gradient of something approaching one in four.

Once more the line is formed, extending some four hundred yards in from the track. Unless the woodcock have lost all sense of decency everyone will get some shooting as we move downhill. Actual connections will be another matter entirely. If the day is fine and dry the first twenty minutes are likely to be lively until we meet the denser stands of trees. It will probably be about 4pm by the time that we get back to the cars.

Then it is decision time again. The day traditionally ends with a duck flight and the question is where to go. Six or more are too many for one place so we must split up into groups. One group will probably try their luck at a newly formed flash, the other at a pond. Chances are that one of our company has been feeding a pond all week. These wet places that we will visit are near or in the forest which means that there will be the inevitable movement of woodcock in the early dusk. Being, of course, respectable and law abiding citizens, we will watch them pass without raising our guns and quietly curse that uncaring officialdom whose actions have deprived us of the sport of our fathers.

If harsh December frost improves prospects for woodcock, it can

also do the duck shooting a power of good. With one proviso. The shooting
territory must be generously endowed with running water in the form of
small rivers and streams and spring-fed ponds. Readers may suspect that
we are just a little spoiled in this neck of the woods. Within two miles of
where I write there are some half dozen weedy streams and a couple of
spring-fed ponds. Until the frosts come they are at best unpredictable; an
early morning walk may produce nothing more than the old mallard or a
couple of snipe. But, given two or three nights of sub-zero temperatures,
the script can change dramatically. Opportunities occur at dawn and
dusk with individual streams being better at one end of the day rather
than the other. What I call the dawn streams tend to be narrow places
where duck can be walked up rather than flighted. The evening streams
are those that break out at intervals into ponds or marshy areas, places
that mallard and teal find irresistible in the fading light.

The dawn streams can carry a surprising number of duck if the
temperature is low enough, but they suffer from a common problem. The
bark of a shotgun carries to eternity in the frosty stillness of the dawn
air. I have in mind one stream which typifies the situation. It starts, from
the shooting point of view, where it emerges from a pipe under a wide
and busy road. About one hundred yards from the road it becomes very
shallow and for no apparent reason there are always mallard there in
frost. In consequence this is the inevitable first port of call. The banks are
low and without cover so the drill is for two guns to pop in alternately,
about sixty yards apart. One is practically guaranteed a couple of shots.
If the Gods are with us the duck do the decent thing and rise between the
two guns. Over a stretch of no more than eighty yards twenty or thirty
mallard can rise if conditions are right. But there, unfortunately, the good

146

news ends. As a result of those initial shots pack after pack are likely to rise downstream. These will be mainly teal but there could be a sprinkling of mallard with them. The only hope is to crouch down straight away and hope that one of the packs will be foolhardy enough to come tearing up the stream. Just occasionally teal will do just that.

At times duck can be singularly disobliging. This same stream can, on occasions, fail to deliver the goods. Scenario. A late December morning, fingers falling off with the cold, expectations astronomical. Bag — one snipe. This, though, in some perverse way is part of the enjoyment of the chase. If our quarry were always present on demand we might just as well send the dogs to a retirement home and set up a clay pigeon trap in the back garden.

My First Snipe

It was whilst walking this stream one morning that, like Saul on the road to Damascus, I saw the light. The light, in this particular case, was a re-evaluation of my thinking about cartridges and shot size. I grew up with men who knew of only one cartridge, an Eley No. 4. So ingrained in them was the use of this particular cartridge that anything else was viewed with grave suspicion. Looking back I think that their lifelong affair with the Eley No. 4 had a simple explanation. In those days in rural Ireland we bought our cartridges at the local hardware store and these were the only cartridges that they stocked. I suppose that there were never any complaints about them so the proprietor simply ordered more of the same. Those cartridges, if memory serves me correctly, were manufactured at the time in Galway. I can still remember the day on which I shot my first snipe, a most unlucky bird that succumbed to the said Eley No. 4 at a range of no more than twenty yards.

Some years later, in a fit of reckless abandon, the local hardware store began to give us the option of an Eley No. 5. I suspect that they had been delivered by mistake. For some the end of the world had arrived. Not long afterwards all manner of strange cartridges began to appear on the shelf behind the counter, some covered with weird and indecipherable words. At about this time I was developing a lifelong love affair with snipe shooting. I acquired a box of Russian cartridges which, I was assured, contained No. 7 shot. My degree of success with the snipe jumped immediately with the addition of these magnificent cartridges to my armoury. One frosty morning I was walking the stream when, after several hundred yards, despite ideal conditions, it was clear that the duck had chosen alternative quarters for the day. Not so much as a single snipe took to the air. Usually there will be a few of them there when the ground is hard with frost, often tucked in under a grassy overhang. I was about to abandon proceedings when, in the middle distance, a single drake mallard rose complaining noisily at being disturbed. Intuitively the gun came to my shoulder. But then some part of my inherent radar system told me that the bird was too far out. I lowered the gun. Next, what I can only describe as madness took over. I threw up the gun a second time and fired. The drake fell dead at a distance of some seventy paces. Probably a total fluke but from that day forth my cartridge has always been a No. 7, sometimes a No. 7 ½ if I cannot get the 7. For snipe, golden plover and woodcock I find the 28 gram load ideal but I use a slightly heavier charge of shot for duck, grouse and pheasants.

Our best evening stream in frosty weather was undoubtedly one that ran the length of a long valley with a mixture of farmland and furze-covered hills on either side. Until about three years ago there was a stretch of this stream, some hundred yards plus in length, where it broadened to a width varying between ten and fifteen yards. Adjoining this particular part of the stream was a rushy field covering about two acres. Small hollows in this field held water for much of the winter. A furze-covered hill completed the scenery on one side whilst there were low-lying green fields on the other side. Once the frosts came in December this was the only place to be at dusk. The stream runs almost due east/west and the river Suir, which it eventually reaches by some circuitous underground route, is to the west. It was important to get to this spot early in times of heavy frost because the teal packs would leave the Suir well before dusk and follow the stream searching for nocturnal feeding places.

A few stunted and well-separated bushes on the very bank of the stream provided the only cover. The surrounding ground was quite swampy and it was necessary to wear waders to get to these bushes. We used to crouch in behind the bushes and face the crimson western sky. On a very cold evening it would seem to have an orange glow, probably the last residue of the setting sun. There would still be a brightness in the sky when the first teal appeared. Already a few snipe would have 'plopped' in. We might well put a few in the bag. They are never easy shooting in this particular situation and, in my estimation, a man who can knock incoming, diving snipe with any degree of regularity is rather more than a fair shot.

As is often the case with teal, especially when they are flying low, one tends to hear them before one sees them. Some have the infuriating habit of landing on the water before one picks them up. Early on it is mostly single birds that tend to come. Then, in the gathering gloom, packs of half a dozen, a dozen or even more swish in. Frosty nights mean an absence of cloud cover and as a result the teal can suddenly appear almost out of nowhere. Should they pitch in the only option is to flush them immediately and hope that one can get a glimpse of them before they are lost into the darkness. A few mallard are likely to come too. But, being cagey creatures by this time of year, they will come late and we will be lucky if we see them before they land. In this particular spot there were always long-eared owls in the air at dusk and on more than one occasion they were lucky to escape unharmed. When the mind is firmly set on duck any black object in the sky can cause a reflex response.

I have never seen an owl taking a duck but I am inclined to the view they pick up the odd unwary teal. During the years that we were breeding red-legs our pens were frequently visited by long eared owls. The top of the breeding pens was composed of a triple layer of plastic strawberry netting and on a number of occasions we saw an owl colliding with this netting at dusk, presumably as it hoped to catch a meal of partridge.

Because a lot of the teal tended to come in when it was quite dark we never shot really big bags on that particular stream. Looking back through my diaries I note that I once shot ten by myself and on another occasion eight. But, much more commonly, a few of us would account for six or seven birds.

That very special place is now no more. At least as far as evening flight is concerned. Three summers ago a monster digger appeared and promptly lowered the bed of the stream by the best part of six feet. Within months the rushy field had dried out and was reseeded. The green sward now covering it betrays nothing of the exciting place it once was. The furze on the hill is gone too. Progress, I believe, is what it is called.

Long ago on a farm in another part of Tipperary where my mother was born there was a small field, somewhere between two and three acres in extent, which contained a number of springs. All through the year water would bubble to the surface from these springs causing the whole field to be marshy. There were a few treacherous spots which shook and wobbled if one stood on them. In the 1950s a dam was constructed at one end of the field in order to develop a permanent water supply to the house and yards. The effect of building the dam was to create a water body which varied in area between a half acre and an acre according to the time of year. Since the water was always moving it never froze. During periods of hard frost, teal and a mixture of other ducks poured in. It was a wonderful place to shoot and there was plenty of cover. Once the dam had been built, cattle were excluded from the field and, as a result, every sort of wetland tree and shrub took over. There was one particularly heavy patch of bushes on one side of the water which was no more than ten yards from the edge. It provided perfect concealment. From a different age there were still a few milking stools left in an outhouse on the farm. Before the coming of the milking machine any man worth his salt would milk six cows before breakfast perched on one of these three–legged contraptions. They were surprisingly light and I always took one with me when I went down for evening flight. Snipe, as usual, would bomb in first, then the teal and mallard.

In the early 1960s, during a long period of extraordinarily severe frost, duck could quite literally not be shot out of the place. One evening, quite late on in the flight, I assumed that the dog was bringing in another mallard until, as he approached me, it was clear that the duck was far too white to be a mallard. It was in fact a drake shoveler, the first that I had seen there. I shot two more of them that evening. As I had a suspicion that we had not picked up all that was shot I went back early next morning. There on the water, in addition to a few teal, was a flock of over twenty shoveler. During that cold spell they came and went a few times and we shot several more. Once the frost broke they left us and we never again saw a shoveler there.

In yet another corner of Tipperary the Suir flows leisurely through a low-lying valley. Come the high water of winter a number of meadows along the valley flood on a regular basis. Of a wet year the water may lie for weeks on end. Wigeon and teal frequent this valley in good numbers,

The view across our bog towards the Galtee mountains: real stamina and a good sense of balance is needed to get through it. But the struggle is usually rewarded.

mallard are usually less in evidence but a few will usually put in an appearance well after the light has failed.

Shoveler come too but their appearances are spasmodic. Usually two or three is the most that one sees. I have never seen diving duck here except for one lone pochard who appeared after a very stormy night. I assume that the grassy shallows are not to their liking. When the floodwaters freeze some of the duck move onto the river, especially at one point where it forms a broad bend. The remainder make for the sea which is not too far distant. In one of the flooded meadows the water never freezes because, like that little field at my mother's home place, it is liberally endowed with springs. It is a reasonable large field, somewhere around seven acres, but under normal conditions its water holds very little attraction for ducks. But, when all around is frozen, it really comes into its own. If left undisturbed in frosty weather, a somewhat rare event it has to be admitted, a positive cacophony of sound begins to emanate from it as the light fails. Lapwings and whooper swans are usually first to arrive.

Then, predictably, the teal come in great numbers. What is special about this field though is the fact that it seems to attract all the wigeon remaining in the area. Hungry, after a cold day spent roosting on the river, they are not that easily deterred and contrary to their normal December form, will come in again and again even when volleys of shotgun fire split the icy stillness of the air.

Before the banks were cleared of bushes it was possible to creep up to the broad bend on a frosty morning. Then, a hundred or more wigeon could lift in unison as soon as one made oneself visible. One morning I shot a hen wigeon at this spot. Still alive it glided low in the water towards the opposite bank. My second barrel at no more than forty yards failed to slow its progress. It is quite extraordinary how difficult it can be to kill a wounded bird on the water. To compound matters the dog refused point blank to go into the river. He had already had a couple of retrieves up-river and I think that he had decided that he had had quite enough of total immersions in very cold water for one day. There was, in consequence, nothing for it but to follow the bank down to the next bridge and walk up the other side . This involved a total journey of about a mile. When I reached the point at which the wigeon had made landfall I quickly realised that my detour had been a wasted one. A trail of feathers and a liberal scattering of blood led to an otter's hole in the bank. This was the only occasion in my experience on which an otter took a wounded bird. I have no doubt in my mind but that it was an otter that was the culprit as this was back in the Sixties when the spread of mink across the country had only just begun.

Much nearer to home, in fact less than half a mile away, is a small pond fed by a stream which usually only flows in winter and early spring. If the summer has been wet there is always the chance of a mallard or two here in September. However, most years it is usually well into the autumn before any water begins to accumulate. It is not a

Time for a late breakfast.

particularly attractive pond for duck but a central raised bed of weeds provides roosting for snipe. Once again this is a place that changes quite dramatically in times of heavy frost. Teal, which rarely use it otherwise, can flock in when darkness comes.

On more than one occasion I have committed the cardinal sin of taking too few cartridges. Usually it is a case of stuffing a fistful into the jacket pocket just before rushing to the pond to get in position in time for dusk. My best night there provided seven mallard, two teal and a snipe. And the duck were still coming in when I left prematurely, having run out of ammunition.

In a Tipperary winter it is the inevitable wind and rain that finally sweeps away the frost. Waterfowl respond very quickly to the changing conditions and, before the frost has half gone, the streams and spring-fed ponds have been deserted. Many will see no more than the odd duck until the next batch of hard weather.

The emphasis now changes to shooting over flooded fields and isolated splashes. December river levels are mainly on the high side and it does not take a lot of rain to make the rivers burst their banks. Like mallard finding stubbles before the combine has left the field, duck in general find fresh flood-water very quickly. Wigeon enjoy the shallow areas where they can graze on the just-submerged grasses. Mallard, I suspect, being birds that will eat literally anything, find all sorts of invertebrates that have been displaced from their homes in the soil as water filters into it. In my experience the best shooting is obtained over fresh floodwater as long as it is not too deep. Then, usually sooner rather than later, the duck

151

are off in search of pastures new. This is partly due to the disturbance factor. Everyone knows the initial best spots when the river bursts its banks and makes a beeline for them. As well as this, the accumulations of water soon grow stale and the submerged vegetation dies back and loses its palatability. Earthworms and other small invertebrates displaced by the water are quickly gobbled up or begin to putrefy.

Sometimes, if the weather remains wet and flood levels stay high, the role of water meadows can change. Instead of being nocturnal feeding places they become daytime roosts, especially in areas that are relatively secluded. This helps to explain one of the great letdowns we all experience from time to time. Going down to one of these places in the hour before dusk the heart beat quickens when one sees a positive cloud of duck lifting from the water. When the light fails the shooting will surely be superb! But, as dusk turns to pitch black, it becomes slowly obvious that they are not coming back.

Very shallow floodwaters tend to remain attractive for longer. This, I think, is because much of the grass stays above the surface and is thus less apt to die off. In my experience wigeon can continue coming even after the bulk of the water has drained away. During times of heavy flooding the best of the shooting is often over isolated and comparatively small flashes. It can be quite staggering just how many teal or wigeon will flight into one of these. There is a dairy farm near here which is devoid of

A January scene in our bog. Teal will, hopefully, find the splashes irresistible.

152

cover; essentially one gigantic field divided up into paddocks by electric fencing. At one point, near a farm road, there are two almost adjoining depressions that fill after heavy rain. We are talking of comparatively few square yards of water surface, yet some evenings, in excess of fifty teal may come in. Very late on, a pair of mallard may come as well. I never shoot more than two or three teal here because of the dearth of cover. All one can do is crouch with ones back to a fencing stake and hope that a few of the visiting duck suffer from myopia.

Around the period of the full moon a new dimension opens for the duck shooter. But, it must be admitted, inland waters are rather less predictable than coastal ones. To some extent this is because one is reliant on a fairly big acreage of floodwater. Whilst duck, especially teal and mallard, will come into a pond under the moon, it can be a long time after dusk has fallen and demands a patient wait for, perhaps, no more than a shot or two. Floodwaters provide a different proposition and, given sufficient acreage, there is the potential for a prolonged flight. I have, on occasions, shot wigeon until two or three in the morning. Even in the lulls between the coming of the wigeon packs, all manner of birds are on the move to keep one entertained. Swans, gulls, lapwings and herons cross the sky or call from their feeding spots. An otter may swim by or an owl may flap lazily along the water's edge. Most years it is not until December that sufficient water is lying to make such a foray worthwhile.

I think that for most fowlers there is something special about flighting under the moon. For a few hours one enters and becomes part of a very different world. Wet places become transformed from their familiar and reassuring appearance of the daylight hours to a magic world which few humans bother to enter. Given light, fleecy clouds and a bit of a breeze there is always the chance of making a good bag. Wigeon, in particular, become restless in moonlight and are often on the move throughout the hours of darkness. The only downside is that, should there be roosting water in the area, dawn flight becomes a much less predictable business as, having fed well, wigeon may decide to return long before daybreak.

The Christmas Shoot

No mention of December shooting would be complete without mention of Christmas. Maybe things are different in other parts of the country but in this area of Tipperary shooting on Christmas morning has taken place for very many years. This is in sharp contrast to what prevails in a lot of European countries where the guns stay silent until St. Stephen's Day, or Boxing Day as it is called on the other side of the Irish Sea.

In my early shooting days events surrounding Christmas followed a tried and trusted pathway. Midnight Mass was the real beginning of the festive season. It probably sounds heretical but we always attended in order that the morning would then be free for the traditional outing with dog and gun. Nowadays Midnight Mass has, sadly, been abandoned in favour of an earlier hour.

No one has ever explained to me why this very special Mass has been brought forward to around 8pm. Maybe priests no longer want to stay up into the wee hours. Or again, maybe they are afraid that the Faithful will no longer attend at midnight.

We would get home from Midnight Mass about 1am. Sustenance was then essential for the labours that lay ahead. Such sustenance usually took the form of an enormous fry-up. A card school then commenced. Twenty five was the game, sometimes forty five but this latter was never really favoured because everyone kept forgetting the count. To start off the stakes were likely to be exceedingly modest, perhaps a shilling or two. A shilling became five new pence for those too young to recall the good old days. Then, as the night wore on, the stakes would surely rise, gradually at first then dangerously as dawn approached. I remember one especially happy Christmas when I started by losing shilling after shilling but then started to win fiver after fiver as the night wore on.

In many households there was an elderly relative who would just sit and watch, amazed at the extravagance of those of half his age or less. With the wisdom of age he might participate in the early exchanges. Then having pulled out before matters got too serious he would minister to the refreshment needs of the combatants.

Those Christmas night card schools had a habit of ending rather like a Monopoly game. Someone would win everything and the rest would rue the fact that they had not gone to bed like good Christians at a civilized hour.

Eventually, with the first light of dawn streaking through the window, the game would break up. Lesser mortals, bleary eyed and usually broke, would head for the bed. Hardier men, and those fortified by substantial financial gain, would make for the kitchen. There, anything capable of being fried, to say nothing of things not normally considered for the frying pan, were duly fried.

Alas those nights are no more. The 'box' now provides in-house entertainment to the detriment of conversation and vast amounts of alcoholic beverages of every description are consumed, frequently and at an alarming rate.

The shooting on Christmas morning rarely started too early and usually did not last too long, a couple of hours were about par for this particular sortie. But it was an honourable tradition and one which we will always maintain. Often as not we knew where there was a crafty cock pheasant and he had been granted safe passage until this appointed day. Chances were that he would survive to fly another day. Standards of marksmanship, following a night of something approaching revelry, tended to vary between very poor and quite appalling. Realistically, any bird that found its way into the bag on Christmas morning had every reason to consider itself hard done by. Over the years my contribution to the bag would tend to average out at a single snipe.

Soon after midday we would be back in the proverbial bosom of the family. Food and more food was then the order of the day. But tomorrow, St. Stephen's Day, will be a very different matter. All going well it will be spent tramping the high forests and glens, in pursuit of woodock. The first few hours will be the worst. There is nothing like the mountain to make one regret the excesses of the festive season.

The Fickle Month of January

From the shooting viewpoint January can be, without any shadow of a doubt, the most fickle month of the season. In the course of its thirty one days it is possible to encounter the total meteorological experience. There will be at least one storm, probably two or three, a few days at least of hard frost and, not uncommonly, one or two balmy days towards the end of the month. Given such variety of weather, rough shooting can vary between the sublime and the disastrous. On balance, in recent years, the sublime has been heavily outweighed by the disastrous.

Stormy weather should auger well for the inland duck shooter in so far as its forces fowl away from the ferocity of the sea. It also provides exciting shooting as the duck are tossed about in the evening sky. But there is one big downside. By January the soils of the low-lying meadows are well and truly saturated and it does not take too much wet weather to produce an outsize flood. Quite simply, the aftermath of a storm is, almost inevitably, too much water and too many places for ducks to go. Again, because of soil saturation, floodwaters are usually slow to recede as the precious days of January slip away. But just once in a while one hits on a good spot for evening flight and the disaster days are quickly forgotten.

If there is to be snow, an increasingly rare event, then it is in January

ABOVE
Bailey bringing
back a snipe.

155

that it will come. In this part of Tipperary we rarely see much snow before the turn of the year, other, that is, than on the mountain tops. In shooting terms a combination of snow and frost is all but guaranteed to deliver the goods. Woodcock are forced down from their mountain retreats and are likely to be flushed from damp sheltered corners where the overhang of bushes insulates the ground from the full ferocity of the frost. Only under such conditions is one likely to make a bag of woodcock on ordinary farmland.

Snow and frost also concentrate the minds of golden plover. In the aftermath of flooding, many of them have left the ploughed ground to partake of Nature's bounty that becomes available as the water recedes. There is nothing like a good belt of frost to bring them back to the ploughed sod. On a really cold morning when the rising sun causes the frozen ground to sparkle they can be seen in massed, brown ranks, sometimes in the company of lapwings. They will stay around as long as the frost stays but, given any hint of mildness, they will depart once again for the water meadows.

Should the January weather turn mild, not an uncommon event as the month draws to a close, migrant wildfowl quickly begin to disappear. Ponds and streams which, only a week or two before, hosted handy numbers of teal may now have nothing more on offer than the occasional snipe. One benefit though of those first balmy days of the new year is that they encourage woodcock to leave the forests and lie out in heather and bracken. Now there are opportunities not be missed. Instead of the half chances as birds disappear through a maze of trees or scrub, the shooting becomes more straightforward. Woodcock still provide a challenge though. When flushed in open country they can accelerate away with every bit as much zip as the best of snipe. I enjoy those final days on the hill because there will be good scattering of snipe in the damp patches which add variety to the proceedings.

In the latter days of January I usually bag a few cock pheasants whilst snipe shooting. I think that I owe these to the fact that those whose primary love is pheasant shooting tend to put away their guns soon after Christmas. The result is that, in the absence of regular disturbance, pheasants soon lose that edge which kept them alive during the high shooting pressure months of November and December. Canny cocks which spent the winter in the security of haggards and other places of sanctuary tend to wander out into the surrounding countryside. One sees much the same in February as the increasing day length produces an upsurge in testosterone levels and they begin to wander far and wide in search of prospective soul mates.

PERVERSITY OF THE WOODCOCK

Early January is really all about woodcock for us. By now the wintering population is at its highest. The only problem, and one which should never be underestimated, is the difficulty of finding them. There is something of Will o' the Wisp about woodcock: here one day, gone the next. On windy days, for example, they should be lying up in deep, dry cover on the sheltered sides of hills and forests. But, with the perversity of their kind, they are quite likely to ignore such comforts and spend the days in places where we would never think of searching for them.

Some years ago my sons and I were invited to spend New Year's Day in pursuit of woodcock in County Mayo. Such was an invitation that could not be refused for there are few better places in Ireland to hunt these elusive inhabitants of the wild places. In order to get in a full day's shooting we travelled the night before, a journey of some 150 miles. Everything augured well for the morrow when we left the house at around 6pm on New Year's Eve. The

Field edges are always worth flushing with a gundog, both for pheasant and woodcock.

temperature had held around freezing all day and was dropping rapidly as we set out. With nothing else on my mind other than the prospects for the morrow I was driving at a goodly speed towards Limerick when one of my sons posed a question: 'Why are all the cars coming against us travelling so slowly?'. Pulling in to a layby I put a foot out onto the tarmac and immediately discovered the reason for the caution being shown by every motorist other than myself. The road along which we had been travelling was covered with a sheet of black ice. Only by the grace of God, since I had been doing well in excess of seventy miles per hour, had we escaped going through a ditch. The consequence was that a journey that normally takes about three-and-a-half hours took nearly double that time. It was past midnight by the time that we reached Castlebar and there were still a few more miles to travel. Not to worry though, great things beckoned for the dawn. Getting out of the car however, having at long last reached our destination, the first seeds of doubt were sown. It did not seem too cold and, ominously, a breeze was stirring from the west.

On entering our host's house however woodcock were temporarily forgotten. A great characteristic of the Irish shooting man is that he never fails to lavish the good things of life upon his guests. I can honestly say that I have never left the home of a kindred spirit without having been well dined and even better whiskied. (Well, if one can be wined I assume that one can, with equal grammatical accuracy, be whiskied). Our host that night was no exception, nor for that matter was his good lady wife. Shooters' wives rarely get the credit that they deserve. They are deserted

for long periods during the winter months, they are expected to come up with large quantities of sandwiches at short notice and they are expected to feed large and ravenous hordes who descend upon their home without any warning.

Twilight at the flight pond in the bog. Note the gently-sloping feeding bank on the island.

That night we partook liberally of the fruit of the grain, some might say too liberally for it was well after three before we made our way to bed. By now the wind had risen quite considerably and gusts were spattering the window panes with sizeable drops of rain. Not to worry though, this was just another Atlantic squall which would blow itself out in a few hours, or so I thought as I drifted off into a deep, ethanol-induced sleep.

Rising early it seemed that our meteorological prediction had been correct. The rain had stopped and the wind had died. Soon after daybreak we were out in pursuit of woodcock. It was a fine, mild morning and just a touch soggy underfoot. The day was to have, however, a rather less than auspicious start. Passing a rushy patch, one of my sons enquired of our host as to whether it might yield a snipe or two. Receiving an affirmative reply he proceeded to walk into the rushes and immediately sank to his waist in an oozy, black quagmire. As he sank a single jack snipe fluttered into the air. To his credit he shot it on his way down. No easy feat to swing a gun upwards when one is travelling rapidly in the opposite direction.

The next hour or so provided some great shooting. We were in a vast area of scrub and small patches of woodland. Literally every piece of cover held the promise of woodcock. The springers applied their trade with customary zeal and it was not long before we had six birds in the bag. Then, abruptly, everything changed dramatically. Evil, black clouds swept in from the west and within minutes we were soaked to the skin despite our allegedly waterproof gear. When it rains in Mayo it does so seriously. There was nothing for it but an about-turn and make for the car for a change of clothes. On the way back we added another bird to the bag in the spilling rain. Then, having changed, all we could do was sit mournfully in the cars as the rain continued to fall in buckets. Decision time soon arrived as the weather showed absolutely no sign of improving. Would we abandon proceedings or take another soaking in the hope of bagging a few more birds? There was really only one answer. Driven by that slightly mad streak which lurks in the soul of all rough-shooters, we set out again. Not far from the cars we came to an almost circular clump of hazels which extended to nearly half an acre. As we approached it our host told us that a fortnight previously (they only shoot each patch at this interval) it had delivered eleven woodcock. This time only two obliged and fell almost together as my son and I fired. Our host, not realising that the two of us had fired, came over to congratulate me on the sheer speed of my right and left.

I was immediately reminded of another shoot which the same son and I had attended some years earlier. It was a duck shoot and birds had flown high and well all morning. Near the end of the shoot three mallard crossed almost directly overhead and at maximum height. As on this day in Mayo we fired almost simultaneously and two of the mallard folded. After the shoot I was congratulated by all who saw the event. One man went so far as to tell me that in a long life spent shooting he had never seen a faster right and left. I should, I suppose, have owned up but reputations are hard to earn and this was just too good a chance.

A Memorable Bird

Despite the driving rain we shot on until lunch time and then, once again, had to return to the cars. We drove back to our host's home where that great lady of the house provided us with another set of clothes. Then, after a quick meal, and driven on by that same mad streak to which I have referred, we set out again. Despite the atrocious conditions we succeeded in shooting a few more woodcock. The final bird of the day will remain long in my memory. Emerging from some particularly dense and dripping scrub we encountered a magnificently manicured football field, complete with neat white railings. Along our side of the field ran a drain which our host jumped ahead of me. In so doing he flushed a woodcock from the only patch of vegetation in the drain. As it flew low across the field our host dived for the ground shouting 'Shoot it!' After momentary hesitation, I felt that it would be a little on the ungrateful side to plant a few grains in his backside, I dropped the bird in almost the centre of the field.

Dusk was now falling rapidly and we were again soaked to the skin. But it had been a wonderful day's shooting despite the inclement weather and being wet was an insignificant price to pay. The only problem was that the supply of dry clothes was now exhausted and there was nothing for it but to eat a fine repast in steaming gear and set off on the long road back to Tipperary. Despite probably the worst conditions under which I had ever spent rough shooting we ended up with fourteen woodcock, two snipe and the jack snipe.

Two days later the January weather, as is its wont, changed once more and we were back to heavy night frosts. It was getting near the end of the Christmas holidays but we still had a couple of days of freedom. What more natural therefore than a trip to the forest for another crack at the woodcock? Unusually, the frost had penetrated the forest and the ground was rock hard. Woodcock were conspicuous by their absence. A couple of hours of searching failed to reveal as much as a single bird. But there was one last chance and it proved to be a winner. Running down one side of the forest is a tumbling stream well shrouded with vegetation on either bank. We decided to walk it down from the high ground. This meant a stiff climb to where the stream rises from a small, spring fed pond some eight hundred feet up in the mountain. As we followed the stream down, the ever-eager springers flushed woodcock after woodcock from the bracken that adorned the banks. It would be nice to say that the bag was filled once again. But this was not the case. My excuse was that the cold air had given me a raging toothache. I did not enquire of the sons who would normally deal with woodcock with quiet efficiency. To be brutally frank we all shot atrociously. Having flushed in excess of a dozen birds we succeeded in knocking only two. To add insult to injury one of these fell into the stream and was washed away unnoticed by the dogs.

I have a relative who farms not too far from the sea in County Waterford. His land is given over exclusively to tillage but it is a place that I rarely visit. No reflection, be assured, on the good man himself. It is just that it is a rather bleak piece of land, almost completely devoid of cover and which, in consequence, has little attraction for game. Even the sugar beet, of which he grows some forty acres, never seems to hold more than the very odd pheasant. Long ago we would meet the occasional covey of grey partridges there but they have long since disappeared from that part of the county.

Just once in a while I get a phone call from this good gentleman. And when he does phone it is not a call to be ignored. He only phones if something special is happening and the inference is always crystal clear. Drop everything and get there quickly. Very many years ago, when it was still permissible to shoot the white-fronted goose, he rang to tell me that they were coming into a beet field and making a proper mess of it. Exceptionally heavy rain had reduced the field to the status of a bog and he was, unsurprisingly, rather less than happy about it. In an earlier chapter I promised that I would write no more of the wild geese and that remains my intent. Suffice to say that we lay out between the drills of beet on a moon-lit night and enjoyed a memorable goose flight. Long before the geese came that night, mallard and teal descended upon the field in awesome numbers. The temptation to shoot them was hard to resist but the geese were going to come and nothing was going to jeopardize the chance of a good bag of them.

WHITE-FRONTS IN THE BEET

Until that night I had never associated geese with beet. It was years later that I learned that the crop is specially grown to hold them in some sanctuary areas. Scientists, apparently, like to refer to it in such places as a sacrificial crop. Having seen the devastation in my relative's beet field I would consider that a rather more than appropriate term. Parts of the field had been reduced to the proportions of a rubbish tip. Bits of beet leaves and chunks of roots were strewn all over the place. If memory serves correctly he was lucky to get what was salvageable of the crop out of the field in early February. In those days, despite the best efforts of four beet factories, the campaign went on well into the new year. Nowadays there is just one beet processing plant and it seems to wrap up its operation about Christmas time. Marvels of modern science.

A lot of years passed before I received another call from this part of County Waterford. It was in the middle of January and again, it was around the time of the full moon. My relative phoned very early one morning, it was scarcely light, and he had some exciting news. He had been awakened early by a combination of moonlight flooding through the bedroom window and an extraordinary volume of noise coming from the field in which we had shot the white-fronts some years previously. Being unable to go back to sleep he decided to get up and investigate the noise. He told me that on going down to the field the biggest flock of duck that he had ever seen took off. The field was in stubble, the aftermath of a crop of winter wheat, and there were several pools of water there. I have never understood why this particular field holds water; it is the only one on the farm that does. It is not appreciably lower and appears quite flat. Maybe in times long ago generations of cattle had pounded the ground in certain feeding areas and created something of a pan. The compressed soil, which can be a couple of feet beneath the surface, prevents the water from draining away.

What surprised me was the fact that the field contained wheaten stubble, and was still attracting birds so many months after the harvest. Duck generally much prefer barley stubble and there is little feeding usually left after October. I can only think of a handful of occasions on which I shot duck over stubble in winter. Much the same holds true with the pinkfeet in the stubbles of eastern Scotland. By November they begin to move into grassy fields.

Anyway we were not going to look the proverbial gift horse in the mouth. By early afternoon we were inspecting the field. Parts of it were quite dry but there was a considerable amount of water lying in pools no more than two or three inches deep. Mallard feathers were very much in evidence and there was also plenty of those small spotted teal feathers. Surprisingly, since they are grazing duck and there was little greenery in the field, wigeon had left their calling cards as well. Quite a lot of snipe departed on our arrival but they were obviously very attracted to the place as they began to return almost immediately. This is very unusual for snipe. New arrivals in September and October do return after they have been disturbed but by this time of year they will usually not come back to a favoured spot until dusk.

So nearly a perfect retrieve. What a pity Bailey dropped the snipe at the last moment!

Dusk would come before six but, with the moon well passed first quarter, there would be little duck traffic until a little later. We had, thus, plenty of time to enjoy my relative's customary hospitality and take on board the necessary sustenance for the long hours that we confidently expected to lie ahead.

Predictably, bursting with anticipation, we went down to the field far too early. Since there was no cover the only option was to lie out on the drier parts. As is usual when the moon is shining at dusk, only a few teal moved at first. They saw us easily and never came in range. For what seemed an eternity, but was probably no more than fifteen or twenty minutes, nothing moved save snipe and curlews. Was it possible, we began to wonder, that the duck had moved on to pastures new. The answer, fortunately, was very much in the negative. As the moon rose high the sky filled with large and small duck silhouettes. In the bright moonlight we were rather obvious but sufficient duck passed within range to provide us with the best bag of the season. We shot mainly mallard that night. Only a handful of teal returned and we did not see or hear wigeon. The bag could probably have been a lot bigger, but it is never easy to sit up from a lying position and swing sweetly. Maybe it was just as well that there was no cover. Human beings can be greedy animals and we would almost certainly have shot far too many if we were properly concealed. The following day I opened the crops of some of the slain as I was far from convinced that wheaten grains were the big attraction. My suspicions proved correct. Every crop contained nothing except a tangle of tiny red worms. Like so many of the mysteries of nature I wondered how the mallard had discovered this particular food source.

Six years have passed since that very special night. I have visited the farm a few times but for purely social reasons. It has not since then provided us with any shooting. But hope springs eternal and one day soon, I am convinced, the phone will ring and summon us to a special event once again.

Lure of the Stubbles

In a long, and some would say, misspent life devoted to the pursuit of wildfowl, I have only rarely flighted duck over late winter stubbles. One of those very rare occasions was way back in the early 1960s when winters were still real winters. During a period of intense frost we had discovered that woodcock had taken a liking to mud banks along the edge of a small tributary of the Suir where sallies overhung the banks in great profusion. For a few magical days the shooting was quite brill ant. One of us walked along the middle of the river, the others worked the dogs along the banks. Most of the woodcock flew down the river so the man in the middle was in Paradise. We had just finished one evening, the setting sun was providing a crimson glow in the western sky, when we noticed packs of teal crossing the river less than half a mile away. They were followed by a few pairs of mallard. All of them were heading for a low hill on which there were a number of small stubble fields. In those days there was hardly any winter corn and most of the stubbles were not ploughed until the spring. It was too late to launch an offensive that evening. There are few things more counter-productive than arriving at a flighting destination in the middle of a flight. Plans were quickly laid: we would be on that little hill well before dusk the following evening.

Next day it was still very frosty and everything augured well for the evening. However I was destined to set out alone as my companions of the previous days cried off at lunch time. As per usual I set out far too early and reached the river whilst it was still very bright. Walking along the bank I met a diminutive figure carrying a magnificent Damascus barrelled hammer gun complete with underlever. At most the young man was sixteen years of age. We got into conservation and it quickly became apparent that even at this tender age he had developed a consuming passion for shooting. He had heard us when we were shooting the woodcock the previous day and, thinking that there must be duck on the river, he had come to investigate. I told him about the stubble fields and he jumped at my suggestion that he might like to accompany me. To get to the hill we had to cross the river just a little downstream from where we had shot the woodcock. There had been very little rain and where we made the crossing the water rose no more than half way up our boots.

My thoughts were miles away, centred upon the flight that was to come, when the bang of my companion's gun jerked me back to the present. In front of us the river surface boiled with the shotgun blast. 'Got it,' said he triumphantly. My initial reaction had been that he had stumbled and accidentally discharged his gun. But this was not the case. Threshing in the water was a very large salmon. Before the young white hunter could grab it, it righted itself and made a run for some still water just above our crossing point. It reached a pool some four feet deep, turned over and promptly sank to the bottom. The said hunter was not deterred. He was not going home without his fish. He took off his trousers, hopped into the extremely cold water and retrieved his trophy. They do not make them like that nowadays. Some might say just as well. It was a fine cock fish which must have weighed the best part of twelve pounds. Less anyone might think that we make a habit of shooting salmon I can truthfully record that this was the only one that I ever witnessed being despatched in this manner. Shot usually richochets off water and I think that the only

Surrounding a pond in advance of a duck drive.

reason that this particular fish succumbed was because the water was so shallow. It is not often that one sees a good, clean fish in the small rivers at this time of year. In my experience it is mainly spent fish that one comes across, often looking thoroughly unpleasant as they are covered with fungal growths.

If matters had already started to go downhill that evening, further events did nothing to reverse the trend. The stubble fields were bounded by heavy ditches so cover was not going to be a problem and, judging by the number of birds that we had seen the previous evening, great things lay ahead. It was not to be, however. Not long before dusk a single teal appeared and set off on a precautionary circuit which proved to be the last that it would ever make. And that was it. Such are the vagaries of the pursuit of wild duck.

Walking back to the car I suggested to my new acquaintance that there were more conventional ways of catching fish and that shotguns should be reserved for the pursuit of furry and feathered creatures. I don't think, however, that he took me at all seriously. He was too preoccupied trying to keep his salmon safely under one arm. He then revealed an entrepreneurial streak for one so young. The following morning, he reminded me, was New Year's Day, and that on some rivers this marked the opening of the salmon season. He went on to explain that the first fish of the new season was purchased for big money by an hotel or upmarket restaurant. We are talking several hundred pounds, a not inconsiderable sum in those far off days. It was his intention, he continued, to get it to Dublin by hook or by crook and so get his paws on the money. I put it to him that this was not a good idea. The fish, having received a charge of shot at not much more than ten yards, was probably riddled with pellets. The patrons, I told him, of the aforementioned upmarket restaurant would be less than impressed by a mouthful of lead. But he was undeterred. On reaching the road we parted company and I never saw him again. I have often wondered whether, like his poaching counterparts of former times, he was duly captured and sent to a penal colony in Van Diemen's land to reflect upon his sins.

A SNARED SPENT SALMON

A much more innocent episode with a salmon took place on another January day. We had been hunting the banks of an overgrown mountain stream for woodcock. The stream, which was no more than five or six feet wide, effectively ran under a tunnel formed by thorn bushes. At intervals these bushes extended well out into the heather. The springers had been going about their business with their usual gusto and had flushed a few birds. Suddenly, some hundred yards form where the stream joined a river, pandemonium broke out in the middle of the cover. From the noise it was clear that one of the dogs was in trouble. The bushes were very dense and it was only with considerable difficulty that I was able to crawl in to the site of the yelping. On the very bank of the stream I found the dog caught in a snare. It had obviously been set for a fox and I could only assume that the person who set it had walked up the stream from the river. Whoever he was he had gone to considerable trouble to set the snare in such an unlikely place.

Having freed the springer I discovered that he had not suffered any injury. In fact he immediately took off in pursuit of his companion. I was about to crawl back out of the cover when a slight movement caught my eye. Lying on a nearby shingle bank a large, spent salmon was wriggling its last. It struck me that if I put it in the snare and pulled it tight around the gills it would give the snare's owner some food for thought. It would also earn him a few pints whenever he told his story. So the deed was done. I had intended to return in a couple

Mallard high and wide.

of days to see whether the fish had been removed. As it happened I never got round to it but I would dearly have loved to see the man's face when he came across his 'catch'.

Whilst storms are part and parcel of the January weather scene, really vicious ones such as we sometimes see on our television screens battering the coastline of the southern United States are very much a rarity. Our typical storms in Tipperary involve winds of 50 or 60 miles per hour with gusts into the high 70s. These pale into insignificance when one thinks of those American hurricanes with wind speeds of 150 or more miles per hour. In my lifetime in Ireland I can only remember a handful of really serious storms. Because they are so uncommon they are usually long remembered. The aptly named 'Night of the Big Wind', a January night in 1839, takes pride of place in the history of such occurrences.

The month of January in 1974 provided some extraordinary episodes. There was an afternoon in the middle of that month when I made the quite ridiculous decision (in retrospect) to go snipe shooting. In a moderate-to-strong wind, snipe can provide some great snap shooting. However, a point comes when the strength of the wind is such that shooting becomes impossible. Such is its force that even close rising birds are torn out of range before one can align the gun. Anyway, under such conditions a smooth swing is impossible as the barrels are buffeted by the wind. On that particular day the forecasters had got it about half right. They had indicated wild weather but never prepared us for what was to come to pass later that evening.

The snipe shooting that afternoon, or more correctly the attempted snipe shooting, was scheduled for some nice grassy and slightly damp fields. A longer than usual lunch meant that it was getting on for three before the expedition began. My companion cried off at the last moment; clearly he knew something which I did not know, so it was a solo venture. By the time that I reached the appointed fields the wind had risen quite considerably and the odd gust had sufficient force to make me stagger. Since I weigh a little over fourteen stone readers will appreciate that we are not talking about a gentle summer breeze. The first two snipe to rise

165

were just about manageable. They both rose close but with the strong wind fell a good fifty yards away. Thereafter matters deteriorated rapidly. The wind continued to rise, rain began to fall like the proverbial stair rods and shooting became impossible. Such was the buffeting of the wind that there was no chance of lining up the gun with the snipe which were now rising in good numbers. Then came the final indignity. A massive gust of wind blew me over. Logic, often in short supply amongst dedicated rough shooters, demanded that when a fourteen stone man can no longer stand up in the wind, then it is time to go home. For once I bowed to the inevitable. That night, at the peak of the storm, conditions were quite terrifying for a couple of hours and gave us some insight into what the inhabitants of the hurricane-prone states of America are subject to on a regular basis. I often wonder how people in these places come to terms with the fact that their roofs may disappear overnight.

The remainder of that particular January was mainly wet and windy. Water lay everywhere and, in consequence, duck shooting was poor. Even snipe were hard to come by, not because their numbers were down but because the superabundance of suitable habitat was such as to stretch them thinly over a vast area. Bogs which could normally be relied upon to show a dozen birds or more could provide no more than one or two. Then, as is usual, 31st January arrived too soon.

The day dawned misty and, ominously, breezy with grey-black clouds scudding across the sky. By early afternoon the wind was little short of force eight and giving every indication that it would go considerably stronger. Common sense dictated that it should be an evening for the fireside and the television. And anyway, the countryside was well and truly saturated, with water lying everywhere. But the last evening of the season is the last evening and has to be shown the deference it deserves.

SHOOTING IN FORCE EIGHT

Where to go for the final evening flight, though, was something of a dilemma. I settled upon a cousin's farm where three fields along the river usually provide a few shots when the floods are in. It used to be a fabulous place for wigeon but some years back he cut a deep drain through the centre of the middle field, so now the level of the floodwater rises and falls with the river. More in hope than optimism I set out on the fifteen mile journey knowing that with the river in spate, there would be much more water than would be ideal.

My journey was not without incident. The wind, coming from the southwest, was strong enough to shake the car and tear twigs off oak and ash branches where they overhung the road. Despite the fact that I arrived at my destination a good hour before dusk, a greyness was descending over the countryside. On reaching the flooded fields it was immediately apparent that waders would not get me to my favourite position out in the middle where it is possible to stand with one's back to a heavy ditch.

Red floodwater was swirling in from the river and the only hope

January was wet and windy, making a vast part of the country possible habitat for wildfowl. The signs were everywhere – like these distinctive teal prints in the soft mud.

was to stand by a small clump of bushes at the edge of the highest of the three fields. As it happened this was the optimum position. The wind was coming from directly across the river pulling the flighting duck, which normally follow the course of the river, across to near where I was standing. I was not long in position when a few black knobs in the sky suggested that, after all, the season might just go out with a bang rather than a whimper. The black knobs, for reasons that were totally inexplicable, were leaving the security of a sheltered lake some six miles downstream. Battling into the wind they were making very slow progress. Such was the force of the wind that they were very near before their whistling betrayed their identity. There were numerous small packs on the move, mostly no more than ten or fifteen birds. All were following exactly the same line.

They were no more than twenty yards up and the same distance to my left. It was then that my heart sank. In what I had thought would be a token gesture to the dying season I had not bothered to bring my cartridge belt. Instead I had stuffed a few cartridges into a pocket. Such are the woes of fowling. This was clearly going to be a flight of epic proportions and I had nine cartridges. The first knob of wigeon developed into a wavering line as they passed. Shouldering the gun was, under the circumstances, a challenge in itself. I fired a single shot and the bird next to the one I thought that I was firing at folded and fell. The rest of the wigeon had disappeared into the gloaming before I could even think about a second shot. I will never forget the next shot. This time I succeeded in striking the bird that I had fired at. It stopped for a moment in the air and then, before falling, collided with a neighbouring bird. Off balance, and in by now a howling gale, this second unfortunate bird simply fell out of the sky and landed in the water only feet away from me. This was the only time in my life that I 'captured' a wigeon without actually shooting it. It was still reasonably bright and the wigeon kept coming. Within minutes I had seven in the bag, including the one that had lost its balance. I had also run out of cartridges. I had never before seen so many wigeon passing over me.

But, in some strange way, I did not mind the fact that I could not shoot them. For less than half an hour I was part of a primeval tableau in which the elements at their fiercest battered but did not subdue the creatures of the wild. Strangely, with the exception of a single mallard, I saw no other duck that night. Maybe mallard and teal are a wee bit brighter than wigeon. I had been out at my stand for less than an hour and when the flight finally ended I suddenly realised that the floodwater, which at the start of proceedings was not much above knee level, was getting dangerously near to the top of my waders. If I had stayed much longer I would surely have ended the season in a rather soggy state.

All good things, so it is said, come to an end. The shooting season is no exception but rarely does it finish, at least for me, in the dramatic

A flight of mallard making good their escape.

168

fashion just described. More typically, the weather at the end of January is hinting at spring, daffodils are getting near to flowering and many of the wigeon and teal have left these parts. Only a few snipe remain to remind us of that which is now all-but gone. Most mortals have to respond to the call of the workplace from Monday to Friday or Saturday. In consequence their season has already ended unless the final days happen to fall at a weekend. For this particular mortal, time just has to be found to salute the passing season. At the very least there are a couple of hours at each end of the day.

My final morning pilgrimage usually takes me to a few places of extreme solitude where the last of the teal may still be in residence.

There could also be a few mallard on the quiet ponds and streams but I am disinclined to shoot them. By now they have paired off, indeed some have been in that happy state of connubial bliss since November. If the weather turns mild the lady duck may well start to lay in early February. It would be churlish in the extreme to deny her the right to replenish her kind at the proverbial eleventh hour. It might, I suppose, be argued that the same holds true for teal. But I do not think that this is the case. Few are paired, at least in the conspicuous way of mallard and anyway their minds will not turn to thoughts of procreation for another couple of months. One does meet pairs of teal in late January but, just as often, one meets threes and fours. A couple of teal in the bag and perhaps a snipe or two are about average for this last-morning foray.

The material world will now require my attention until around 4pm. Thereafter it is time for the last round-up. This comes in two parts. Part one is a walk in the haunts of snipe. They have been the mainstay of my shooting for the past five months and it is only right and proper that I pay my respects before we go our separate ways. They will go to wild and rushy places to breed, I will go to address the myriad of tasks in house, garden and farm which have been the subject of near-criminal neglect since the dawning of that first September day. If the day is mild, the snipe may be a little relaxed and, despite months of harassment, allow reasonable approach. But if it is wild and windy they are unlikely to hang around. After the first week of January, days begin to lengthen but even at the end of the month they are still perilously short. This means that after an hour of snipe shooting it is necessary to move to the season's final destination for part two. If the chosen place is far away, the snipe shooting will be little more than a nominal affair.

As with all duck flighting there is a big element of luck in hitting upon the right spot. Last season I found such a spot by pure accident. Some days before the end of January I had been snipe shooting in one of the best rushy bogs in the locality. A winged snipe had carried a couple of hundred yards beyond the bog and pitched in an adjoining field. This field has a few hollows which hold water in winter but I had never seen duck using them. Walking over to retrieve my snipe I noticed that the surrounds of one of the flashes was positively littered with duck feathers. They were mainly teal feathers but a few were mallard. Even better, a second and smaller flash had even more feather floating on the water and in the surrounding grass. It was abundantly clear that duck had been visiting for some time.

The witching hour – when the ducks appear – was not too far off, when one of my sons and I arrived at the flashes on that final evening. There was only one problem. Cover was confined to a reed-filled drain just out of range from the flashes. The direction from which the duck would come would thus be critical.

We had just settled into the drain when three mallard swept over our heads and proceeded to land on the small outer flash without so much as a single precautionary circuit. They were clearly well used to the place as self respecting mallard rarely come in before teal.

169

Almost immediately a single mallard came in from the same direction and joined the three on the water. It was a cloudy evening and the darkness was gathering rapidly when a bunch of teal came in low and fast. Four shots resulted in only two falling. Each of us claimed the pair but we really knew that we had got one each. Then three teal came in and landed before we had time to fire. Finally a single teal appeared and, unlike earlier arrivals, decided to do a circuit. If it had come in like its colleagues it would probably have survived. As it was, two almost simultaneous shots brought its flight to a premature end. And that was that. It was now too dark to continue shooting so there was nothing for it other than to head for home. As we walked back to the car an assortment of duck noises indicated that the wiser birds had opted for the security of real darkness before coming to their evening meal.

Once home it was time for the annual bout of serious melancholy. September seems a long way off. 'I wonder if I'll be here next season?' has become something of a traditional refrain. A long-suffering wife throws her eyes to Heaven and makes for the kitchen or further afield. There is just so much of someone else's melancholy that a person can take.

The Years to Come

The future of game shooting, like that of all fieldsports (note fieldsports and not that scurrilous term bloodsports), is inevitably linked to a number of diverse influences. Amongst these are the already in-train changes: in agriculture and the related issue of land ownership; the worldwide rejection of the use of lead shot; changing attitudes as modern man decides that he is an urban animal rather than a rural one; the fragile goodwill of politicians, the strategies of those who control the destinies of the State's forests and the not unrelated matter of tourist shooting.

Throughout Europe the face of agriculture is changing rapidly. Nowhere is this more true than in Ireland. Historically, few countries were more dependent on agriculture but this has now all changed with the rise of such as the pharmaceutical and information technology industries. Correspondingly, the political clout of the agricultural sector has diminished. The changes taking place will, inevitably, impinge upon game and game shooting. Some will, I believe, impinge in a positive way; others may not be so positive.

The single biggest change in agriculture is, without doubt, the move away from linking support payments to productivity. The new Single Payments Scheme requires only that a farmer keeps his lands in good

Waiting hopefully: the beginning of a snipe drive.

171

ABOVE
A mallard drake, secure in sanctuary water.

order and pays due regard to the requirements of conservation. No longer does he have to put so many acres under cereals or carry so many head of livestock to qualify for support. This just has to be good for game. It will not be necessary, at least in theory, to put the last square metre of land under the plough or graze every rushy pasture down to the quick in order to keep the wolf from the door. Some, of course, will carry on exactly as before. But others, I believe, will take their Single Payments and adopt a rather more relaxed attitude to the business of farming, especially those who already have another job outside the farm. On balance there should be less demand placed upon the natural environment to provide high yields year after year and this should help all forms of wildlife to prosper. In the long term I would have, like all farmers, concern as to whether the Single Payments system will last far into the future. The history of agricultural supports in Europe is a somewhat chequered one. Policies have been apt to change with quite bewildering suddenness. If in say ten years' time, the Single Payment is withdrawn, there could be a return to intensive production as farmers strive to maintain income levels. Should this happen, all the environmental positives could be quickly wiped out.

One aspect of less intensive farming deserves special mention as far as game is concerned. It relates to insect life. From the day that they hatch, young birds must make a rapid spurt to maturity. To do this they must have an abundant supply of protein. The bodies of insects are the prime source of this protein. There is no doubt that insect life has declined in the Irish countryside over the last few decades. This is largely due to the decline in the numbers of host plants which support them. Fields of barley and wheat have become sterile places in which no other plants are tolerated. Equally, the practice of reseeding pastures at regular intervals with hybrid grasses has deprived the meadows of that once wonderful mix of flowering plants. Should these plants make a return, and I think that there is every chance that they will, the pheasant will be a major

RIGHT
Matters such as vermin control must be approached with ever greater diligence if shooters are to continue to enjoy the goodwill of farmers. Here a grey-back has been called to its doom by a magpie.

172

beneficiary. It would be nice to think that this would also hold true for the grey partridge. But, alas, I do not believe that this will be the case. In my view the decline of this noble bird has long since passed the point of no return. On a more positive note, if releases of the red-leg continue, an increased food supply could certainly help to bring about the establishment of a wild population.

Another aspect of the Single Payments scheme that could benefit game is the provision that a farmer can turn over part of his holding to forestry without losing his entitlements. My understanding is that he can plant up to half his acreage with trees. Whilst the purist may have reservations about growing trees on prime agricultural land, it is an exciting proposition for the game preserver, especially if the planting is mainly of deciduous trees. Even a mix with conifers would be immensely beneficial. Unlike the vast spruce monocultures of the State's plantations, farm forests are typically smaller and mixed and therefore more attractive to game. Maybe there is an element of wishful thinking but it is not beyond the realm of possibility that, in a few years' time, woodcock may become regular visitors to parts of the country that, presently, they only visit during periods of severe weather.

Then there is the latest edition of the Rural Environment Protection Scheme, REPS 3 as it is entitled. Whilst I was not fully convinced of the value to wildlife of the earlier schemes, I am much more enthusiastic about the latest version. In particular I like the idea of fencing off a couple of acres for wildlife. Such places can provide havens for refuge and nesting which

have all-too-often been absent in a regime of intensive farming.

On a somewhat different note there is the matter of farm size. A feature of the last few years has been a quite dramatic increase in the size of individual holdings and, in consequence, a reduction in the number of holdings. This could have negative repercussions. Bigger holdings tend to mean bigger fields and a resultant decrease in the availability of cover. As well as this the amalgamation of farms can mean the removal of boundary ditches. These, traditionally, are often dense, tangled affairs much loved by pheasants. Bigger holdings, to state perhaps the obvious, mean that the ownership of sporting rights lies in fewer hands. This could have negative repercussions for the shooting fraternity, as a small number of landowners could, conceivably, preserve a sizeable square of land. It is not uncommon to find that when one man preserves his land, a neighbour follows suit. The clear message for shooters is that they will have to become more receptive to the needs of farmers if they are to continue to enjoy their goodwill. In particular, matters such as crop protection and general vermin control must be approached with ever greater diligence than is presently the case.

MY EXPERIMENTS WITH LEAD SHOT

The use of lead shot for waterfowl shooting is something that will have to be addressed in Ireland sooner rather than later. Indeed, by the time that these lines appear in print, the die may already have been cast. Whether we like it or not the world has turned against the use of lead shot. And it is not merely shotgun pellets that it has turned against. Lead-based paints, lead shot for angling, lead pipes: all have received a definite thumbs down. Lead is toxic, of that there is no doubt. But whether it has, and is having, the devastating effects on waterfowl populations that some claim, is a moot point. And whether the decision to ban it in so many countries is based upon sound science as opposed to simple prejudice or the manoeuvrings of those opposed to our sport is also a moot point. I spent a number of years between 1986 and 1990 trying to assess the situation in Ireland. There have been no massive changes in shooting levels since then so I believe that my findings are still valid today. I will leave readers to decide whether a ban would be justifiable in Ireland when they have considered these findings.

We will start at the beginning. The lead shot debate began in the United States many years ago when it was claimed that a number of large scale wildfowl deaths were attributable to lead poisoning. This precipitated a considerable body of research. Mind you, the sites of these large scale die-offs were mainly where vast numbers of fowl congregated and where they were shot in enormous numbers by commercial hunters intent upon supplying fast-growing communities. I have heard one story, though have never been able to confirm it, that so much lead shot had accumulated in the mud of a particular marsh that it became a viable proposition to extract it. Far-fetched as this may seem, it has to be remembered that when a 32 gram cartridge is fired, several hundred pellets, depending on size, are dispersed into the environment and usually less than half a dozen enter the body of the target bird.

When the spent shot falls over water it quickly sinks to the bottom. What happens next depends upon the nature of the particular water body. If the surface is without turbulence, the pellets are likely to lie on the surface of the underlying mud for a long period of time and thus be available to waterfowl. On the other hand, if the water is moving, silt and stones will soon cover the pellets so that they cannot be picked up.

There has been much debate as to why duck pick up spent shot. Like all birds they need small stones to act as agents of abrasion in their gizzards where food is crushed. Some people believe that duck specifically select pellets for this purpose, mistaking them for small, rounded stones. On balance I believe that this is the most likely reason for the ingestion of spent shot. The alternative is that they mistake the pellets for the seeds of aquatic plants. No doubt this happens to some degree, especially in the case of predominately herbivorous species such as pochard.

Once ingested the pellets pass along the bird's alimentary tract to its gizzard. Here, over weeks or months, the combined action of the crushing process and digestive juices convert the lead to soluble salts which then pass into its bloodstream. These salts of lead are then carried to vital organs such as the kidneys where they cause all manner of problems. A pertinent question is whether the ingestion of a single pellet is likely to have a deleterious effect. This was researched by feeding wild caught birds with a variety of foods to which different numbers of pellets had been added. One study found that a single No. 4 pellet so administered produced mortality levels of 18%-20% in the experimental ducks. Two other similar studies however detected no harmful effects from the ingestion of a single pellet.

During the years that I looked at the situation in Ireland I examined a total of 913 gizzards for the presence of ingested pellets. Of these, 847 were sent to me by gun club members in twenty different counties. Some

Hoping for a woodcock. Woodcock often lurk in cover near the edge of forestry roads.

of these parcels of gizzards had long since passed their sell-by date when they reached me and my postman was somewhat less than impressed. The remaining 66 were kindly made available to me by D.O'Keefe of the Zoology Department of University College, Galway. Since there is always the possibility that a pellet may have been shot-in rather than ingested, it was important to exclude the former category. Fortunately this is not a difficult task. 'Shot-in' pellets deform as they strike bone and other solid tissues and are thus misshapen and tend to have angular edges. In contrast, ingested shot, having been worn down by the action of the gizzard, are typically very smooth. Sometimes one comes across a pellet that has been so worn down that it is less than half the diameter of a number 8.

The Study of Pellets in Gizzards

As would be expected, the biggest number of gizzards that I received came from mallard. There were 371 in all. Teal came in a close second at 294 and wigeon were third at 126. Of the mallard gizzards 11, representing just under 3%, contained ingested pellets. In the case of the teal only three, almost exactly 1%, were contaminated. Only one of the wigeon gizzards contained a pellet. Six of the eleven mallard gizzards contained a single pellet and two more each contained two. Of the remainder one had five pellets and the other two had four each.

It is generally recognised that diving ducks pick up more spent shot than dabblers. This would seem logical in that they have access to the bed of the water body at a great variety of depths whereas mallard and teal feed predominately in shallow waters. Wigeon, being grazers, are the least likely to pick up pellets. In my sample there were 47 pochard gizzards of which 3 contained pellets and 38 tufted duck gizzards of which 2 contained pellets. 2 goldeneye gizzards out of 12 had ingested pellets and 1 scaup gizzard out of 7 was contaminated.

In summary 23 gizzards out of the total of 913 contained pellets and in 15 of these there, was only one pellet. The gizzards were from duck shot at 65 widely separated sites. Only 10 of these sites yielded contaminated gizzards and the few that contained a number of pellets came from the same site. Researchers in the United States use the term 'hot spots' to describe those wetlands which are heavily contaminated with spent shot and which tend to yield gizzards containing many pellets. In my survey there was only one site that might be described as a 'hot spot'.

There is no doubt in my mind that these findings quite clearly indicate that spent lead shot is not a problem of any significance in Ireland. Readers will have to make up their own minds on the issue. Realistically though, in these environmentally sensitive times, a ban will come. Politicians like to appear as friends of the earth. The only questions are when it will come and what form it will take. The main reason why Ireland has not yet moved against lead shot is that the powers that be have something of a dilemma. This centres around the alternatives to lead. For practical purposes we are really talking about steel shot. Strictly this is something of a misnomer as it is really the softest possible iron. Bismuth approaches the nature of lead for ballistic purposes but the cost factor rules it out for the majority of shooters. As is generally well-know, iron is significantly less dense than lead and in order to give it sufficient propulsive force it is necessary to generate much greater pressure in the breech of the gun. I am aware that steel cartridges can be obtained that generate a pressure similar to lead cartridges but I am singularly unimpressed by them. I shot a misfortunate rook with one in the field behind the house. It fell complaining vigorously and proceeded to walk away. I would not consider myself a bad shot but two further blasts of steel did little to slow its progress. I then changed to lead to quickly terminate that particular trial.

It is the higher pressure resulting from the use of steel cartridges which provides the dilemma. Shooting in Ireland is every man's sport, should he wish to participate. Elsewhere it tends to be largely the sport of the wellheeled. Fair enough; there are exceptions as in the wildfowling clubs. But whereas the well-heeled can afford to purchase guns capable of absorbing the higher pressures associated with steel cartridges, ordinary mortals are not all in this fortunate position. Effectively, there are a lot of guns in use in Ireland which are not capable of firing steel cartridges. I am sure that there are even some in use which are decidedly dodgy even for the conventional lead loads.

THE NEED FOR A PROOF HOUSE

If there is to be a ban on lead for some forms of shooting, then gun owners must have a reasonable opportunity to check the proof of their weapons for the higher pressure steel cartridges. Simply stated, they need the services of a proof house. But there has not been one in Ireland for many years so it would be necessary to send guns to an English proof house. Such an operation would be very costly to say nothing of the logistical problem of moving large numbers of guns. Requests have been made for the re-establishment of a proof house, not an unreasonable proposition when it is remembered that there up to 200,000 licenced guns in the country. But so far all requests have fallen on deaf ears. Herein lies officialdom's dilemma. Ban lead and people may start firing steel out of unsuitable guns with potentially calamitous consequences. It would only take one serious accident to precipitate a major political storm.

As to the type of ban, it is my belief that the Scottish model is preferable to what operates in England and Wales. In Scotland the use of lead is prohibited over wetlands but one can still use it to shoot duck and geese in other places. Stubble flighting is the most obvious example. In contrast it is, as far as I am aware, illegal to use lead against duck and geese under any circumstance in England and Wales. This, I think, is unnecessarily restrictive. I would have a serious problem when it comes to defining the types of wetland over which a ban would have to be observed. I shoot snipe over many damp places such as rushy bogs and heather bogs. The great majority of these never see a duck and I doubt whether snipe would pick up spent shot. Snipe gizzards, not surprisingly considering the size of the bird, are tiny organs and difficult enough to examine. I have opened over one hundred and have yet to find a pellet in one. One can only hope that when these matters become the subject of debate and decision, common sense and good science will prevail over prejudice and popular politics. I will not, however, be holding my breath.

THE MORAL DEBATE

Fieldsports enthusiasts live with the fact that their sport involves killing. This is not a problem for them because, being balanced people, they recognise that killing is part of a natural order which has evolved on this planet. This is not to say, however, that the act of killing should be anything but quick and humane. They also have to live with the fact that there will always be a small but vociferous minority which claims that killing in the name of sport is ethically or morally wrong. Strangely, these high-minded people who develop apoplexy at the thought of shooting a pheasant or grouse never seem to get excited about killing a rat or mouse. But they will always be with us. In themselves they are not a problem. Where a problem materializes it is because they can throw all their time and energies at fermenting an anti-hunting ethos amongst ordinary people who hold no strong feelings one way or another in relation to fieldsports. And, like zealots everywhere, they are not too concerned as to whether their propaganda is true or not. Most times it is not.

Amongst country people there is little animosity towards hunting. Living in a rural environment one is much closer to the realities of life and death than are one's urban cousins. Sick animals have to be put down, the cattle lorry from the factory passes each week bearing heifers to their doom, dead rabbits and other traffic victims are an everyday sight on the roads. Even the sad ritual surrounding the passing of a fellow human being is played out in much greater detail in rural communities. But, as people leave their roots to spend their lives in suburbia, they slowly become detached from such scenes. A generation later they can be all too easily seduced by the disturbed outpourings of those fanatics who have seen fit to appoint themselves as custodians of the moral order.

Over the past twenty years or so Ireland has witnessed a very significant movement of people away from the countryside and into towns and cities. There is now hardly a town that is not surrounded by housing estates and, as the population continues to expand, so does the explosion in suburban house building. Even small villages a few miles away from towns have not escaped. Many are in danger of becoming dormitory towns in their own right. This movement or exodus from the countryside could leave country people and their way of life at the tender mercy of an uncaring and ill-informed majority. The fate of fox hunting in Britain, courtesy of a gentleman called Mr. Blair, must send a powerful message to all who love fieldsports in these islands. Mr. Blair, I am sure, would claim to lead one of the finest democracies on earth. To my mind a regime that tramples over the rights of inoffensive minorities foregoes the right to call itself a democracy.

Rural Re-Generation: a Good Sign

There is, however, a hopeful sign beginning to emerge in rural Ireland. The sons and daughters of country people are, increasingly, beginning to build their homes in the countryside. In this area many a farmer's son, who not too many years ago might have moved well away on acquiring a wife, now has his house within a stone's throw of his birth place. Long may this trend continue. The prices being paid for a typical half acre site say it all most eloquently. Much less than a decade ago one could acquire such a site for thirty thousand euro or so. Now asking prices start around fifty thousand and the sky is the limit after that. But Ireland has grown exceedingly wealthy of late and people seem to have little difficulty in coming up with such sums, to say nothing of a couple of hundred thousand more for the construction of a dream house. All of this must be very positive for fieldsports. Thriving rural communities, with an understanding of the ethos of hunting in all its forms, are one of the best guarantees for the future. It is vital that gun clubs, coursing clubs and other like-minded bodies do their best to involve local people in their activities. Organising social events and developing an awareness of the conservation work carried out by hunters are cases in point.

Party Politics and Fieldsports

I like to think of myself as an apolitical animal. But in my heart I know that this is an impossibility for mortal man. We are all creatures of our prejudices and, as such, tend to align ourselves to some part of the political rainbow. My problem is that I have yet to meet a politician who shares all my best prejudices and is also an ardent and outspoken supporter of fieldsports. Irish politics, in contrast to those of most countries of western Europe, are unique in a number of respects. In relation to hunting, shooting and fishing only an insignificant minority of Irish politicians have publicly expressed opposition. Maybe some others share their views but if they do they are far too cute to say so openly. Those that do oppose our sport tend to run in urban constituencies where snipe and woodcock are about as plentiful as virgins. See what I mean about prejudices? It seems to me that the same politicians would be a lot better employed attending to the many problems of their constituents instead of meddling in matters about which they know little or nothing.

In Tipperary our politicians have always been supportive of fieldsports and this is something which I think is generally true throughout much of rural Ireland. Moreover, there is nothing to make me believe that this happy state of affairs is going to change, at least in the foreseeable future. If I were a cynic, I might put forward the thesis that in Ireland there are not too many votes to be obtained by opposing fieldsports but that there are a considerable number to be lost by such action. Of course I am not a cynic.

In most countries there is a perception that fieldsports, or at least some of them, are the prerogative of the upper echelons of society. As such they are regarded as fair game for some of those who espouse the policies of the left. Whatever the Labour Party may care to say in Britain it is abundantly clear that it pushed its anti-hunting bill through parliament for no other reason than simple class prejudice. As I see it there is biologically no difference between chasing a fox and pulling a roach or a rudd out of water. Why did these upright members of the British Labour Party not ban coarse fishing? Easy. It is my understanding that over two million inhabitants of our neighbouring island pull roach and rudd out of water and many of these are supporters of the Labour Party. In all honesty I think that I could easily become a cynic if I tried hard enough.

Incidentally, less there be any misunderstanding, I have no objection whatsoever to coarse fishing. It is another man's sport and good luck to him. The only time that I have caught coarse fish has been by total accident. There is a small lake in County Limerick which I used to fish for trout and which was home to vast numbers of rudd. They always took the fly readily and on a typical evening the ratio of rudd to trout was always around five to one. One evening I had an audience of Boy Scouts who were camping nearby. They were quite clearly amazed at my skill at catching rudd and asked me if they were good to eat. To my eternal shame I told them that they were excellent and they departed with a large bag of them. They never returned for more.

What makes Irish politics unique, more than anything else, is that though on the decline in terms of voter support, the two major parties, Fianna Fail and Fine Gael, evolved out of the Civil War rather than from the usual right/left divide. Over eighty years have elapsed since that sad time when former brothers-in-arms turned against one another and engendered a bitterness which has not yet died. The reality is that these two parties both lie somewhere towards the middle of the political spectrum. So aligned, they are not going to take issue with the fieldsports' traditions in rural Ireland. Even putting to one side their position on the political spectrum, something which is not always easy to ascertain, especially around election time, both parties have roots too well entangled in the townlands and villages of rural Ireland and they are not going to alienate people who are only a generation or two removed from their founding fathers.

The Irish Labour Party is a rather different animal from its British counterpart. Whereas the latter was spawned in the great industrial cities, its Irish counterpart has always had a strong rural base and many of its representatives have a good and supportive understanding of fieldsports. I can honestly say that one of our greatest supporters in Tipperary was the late Michael Ferris of Bansha. Throughout his political career Michael helped us in any way he could. Having met many Labour Party T.D.'s and officials over the years I am of the view that the party does not represent any threat to hunting, shooting or fishing, at least in this generation.

If I have any cause for concern about the future of fieldsports, in so far as politicians are concerned, it centres around the Green Party. Sometime ago I had a long conversation with a senior member of the party. That member told me that they have no problem with rough shooting but draw the line at driven shooting. This is a distinction which is rather too narrow for me and one which, I feel, could all too easily change. Whilst the party is small, and likely to remain so, it could exert influence way beyond its numerical strength in a coalition. It is very unlikely that Ireland will see single party government in the middle term so each of the larger parties will have to seek allies if they are to enter government. Herein lies the danger. Power is the ultimate political prize and who knows what price any party may be prepared to pay to achieve it.

I have always held the view that the shooting fraternity have a lot in common with the Green Party. We share a common concern for the well-being of the natural environment and want to see all wild populations flourish. But whilst I suspect that the thinking of moderates in the party is not too far removed from ours, the matter of killing will always be an insurmountable barrier.

Who Owns the Shooting in Ireland?

The fate of forest and mountain shooting must now be a cause of quite serious concern for local sportsmen. Before the establishment of Coillte some fifteen years ago, clubs or local individuals tended to rent the shooting of these places from the then-Forest and Wildlife Service. Rents were generally low and even though there was a tendering system, a booklet was issued at intervals with the acreages of the various lettings and lists of the likely game species to be encountered. Locals were usually awarded the lettings. When Coillte came into existence it entered periodic agreements with clubs for the lettings that they had traditionally held. This is now changing and it would appear that we are to return to a system of tender.

Commercial interests have been very vocal in relation to the system of agreements. They would claim that they were being denied the right to acquire lettings in some areas because of it. My feelings on this issue are very simple. Local people have an inalienable right to hunt in their own areas. Much of the land now under forestry was purchased from their fathers for very small money. Those same fathers had taken part in the struggle for independence and I am certain sure that when they sold off marginal land they never dreamed that their descendents would be denied the right to hunt over it.

In the legislation that brought Coillte into being certain requirements in relation to conservation were placed upon that body. After all, it was to take charge of a vast estate in the name of the Irish people. I find it very hard to understand how this requirement concerning conservation is honoured when commercial interests are allowed to rent big acreages of prime woodcock terrain in the western counties and shoot them day after day. This is always denied but the simple reality is that the crackle of shotgun fire can be heard on every day of the week. In sharp contrast, club shooters hunt forests only sparingly and pose no threat whatsoever to local woodcock populations. The day has long since passed when migratory birds can be the sole focus of commercial hunting. If people feel the need to make money out of shooting they should, in my estimation, release large numbers of pheasants in their forests and so take the pressure off the migrants. I would go further. I believe that Coillte should insist upon such as part of a lease agreement with commercial operatives. But this is not going to happen. Coillte has one interest, one interest only. The making of money.

WHAT WE CAN DO

I believe that there is an onus on every Irish sportsman to highlight the rape of our forests by these commercial interests and to do all in their power to stop this unacceptable sell-off of our heritage. This means influencing friends, lobbying politicians and writing to newspapers. We owe it to the generations to come.

Then there is the very important matter of the red grouse. Coillte now owns a very considerable amount of heather-covered moorland. It is inconceivable that this species should become the subject of commercial shooting in Ireland. It should be mandatory that any letting to commercial interests excludes grouse shooting. There is no way that the present population could absorb the pressure of commercial hunting.

In fairness to Coillte, and I find it hard to be fair, they have shown some signs of their responsibilities when it comes to grouse. I am aware that a number of clubs have agreements with them to engage in long-term projects aimed at the restoration of the fortunes of this magnificent bird.

I am fully aware that it is easy to be negative about a large commercial concern, which after all, is exactly what Coillte is. I think though that it is important to distinguish between the 'top brass' and the people working at forest level. I know little about the top brass but I have met many of the men who work in the counties. It is right and proper that I pay tribute to them. Almost without exception they understand the local situation and have always done their best for local clubs and for conservation.

My final comments concern the area of tourist shooting. Not the acceptable face of that industry that makes a substantial input in terms of put-and-take species. Rather, I refer to those who sell off our stocks of migratory birds at great profit. In this conservation-conscious age I find it hard to put into words my anger that anyone should see fit to dispose of our natural heritage. Let us make no bones about it, if the present levels of commercial shooting are allowed to continue, the target species will go into decline. Right across the world there are countless examples of what has happened when human avarice has been put ahead of environmental issues. Here in Ireland we have seen a massive decline in the Atlantic salmon because of drift net fishing. If this practice is allowed to continue for much longer there will be no salmon in Irish rivers.

The North American passenger pigeon is probably the best example of what happens to a wild species when mankind decides to profit from it. This was once the most numerous land bird that ever inhabited the earth. The early settlers recorded flocks stretching over a mile in length which darkened the sky as they passed. By the beginning of the twentieth century the species was brought to extinction, primarily by the action of commercial hunters. Habitat loss also played a part, as trees which the birds used for nesting were felled. I think that I once read that the last passenger pigeon in the world died in the Bronx Zoo in 1901.

It must also never be forgotten that Ireland has a very special responsibility in relation to birds such as woodcock and snipe. As western Europe was drained and dried, their wintering haunts were decimated. Ireland, with its mild Atlantic-inspired climate has a vital role to play in the conservation of these species. The relatively light hunting pressures applied by local hunters are not a problem. Seven-day shooting by the clients of the get-rich-quick brigade are another matter entirely.

Game shooting will always be a feature of rural Irish life. Of that I have no doubt. But it is up to this generation to ensure that what we have enjoyed will be available in equal measure to our children and their children. To this end we must remain vigilant and challenge everything which we perceive to be contrary to this simple objective.

I rest my case.

Douglas Butler, May 2006

ALSO PUBLISHED BY MERLIN UNWIN BOOKS

Private Thoughts from a Small Shoot   Laurence Catlow

Confessions of a Shooting Fishing Man   Laurence Catlow

The Shootingman's Bedside Book   BB

Dark Estuary   BB

Tides Ending   BB

Flyfishing in Ireland   Peter O'Reilly

Rivers of Ireland   Peter O'Reilly

Flies of Ireland   Peter O'Reilly

Bright Waters: an anthology of Irish Fishing Writing

www.merlinunwin.co.uk